CORPUS CULTUS IOVIS SABAZII
(CCIS), II

THE OTHER MONUMENTS
AND
LITERARY EVIDENCE

ÉTUDES PRÉLIMINAIRES
AUX RELIGIONS ORIENTALES
DANS L'EMPIRE ROMAIN

PUBLIÉES PAR

M. J. VERMASEREN

TOME CENTIÈME

CORPUS CULTUS IOVIS SABAZII
(CCIS), II

E. N. LANE

THE OTHER MONUMENTS
AND
LITERARY EVIDENCE

LEIDEN
E. J. BRILL
1985

81

CORPUS CULTUS IOVIS SABAZII
(CCIS), II

E. N. LANE

THE OTHER MONUMENTS
AND
LITERARY EVIDENCE

WITH A FRONTISPIECE, ONE FIGURE, 40 PLATES AND A MAP

LEIDEN
E. J. BRILL
1985

ISBN   90 04 07149 0

CONTENTS

PREFACE

In the present monograph I endeavor to present the epigraphical evidence for the cult of Sabazius, together with related monuments, as well as the literary testimonia.

Although it would be entirely possible on the basis of the material presented here to draw numerous conclusions concerning the cult, I have deliberately refrained from doing so, as the presentation of all the evidence, including the hands, is a necessary preliminary for the construction of a complete and sound picture of this religion. A third volume, containing a description of the cult based on the totality of the evidence, is thus also forseen.

The collection of the evidence has been arduous for a variety of reasons. The literary sources, although to a great extent repetitious, uninformative, and obsessed with the ostensible connection between Sabazius and Dionysus, pose the fewest problems. By and large the readings are undisputed, and I have therefore considered it superfluous to indicate in most cases what edition I have used. The epigraphical material, on the other hand, is scattered and in many cases difficult of access. I have collected photographs of the inscriptions, etc., to the greatest extent possible, although in certain cases my quest for illustrative material has remained frustrated.

It is hard to know whom all to thank. The Research Council of the University of Missouri-Columbia gave me travel funds, and the National Endowment for the Humanities a Summer Stipend for 1979, before I went abroad to start collecting material on the spot. The Research Council also generously provided a subvention, without which publication of this volume would have been impossible. The directors and personnel of the following museums and institutions have been most helpful: Deutsches Archäologisches Institut, Abteilung Istanbul; Staatliche Museen zu Berlin (-Ost), Antiken-Sammlung; Kleinasiatische Kommission, Österreichische Akademie der Wissenschaften; Musée National du Louvre; Epigraphiko Mouseio, Athens; Archaeological museums of Thera, Argos, and Epidaurus; Ostia excavations; Musei Capitolini and Museo Nazionale delle Terme, Rome; British Museum, London. Thanks also go to Margarita Tacheva-Hitova, I. I. Russu and C. Petolescu, and Nehad Cambi for help with the Bulgarian, Romanian, and Jugoslav material, respectively. I have many people to thank for help with the photographs, but should single out Michales Chrysinas of Marousi, Greece, for especial mention. Thanks for typing the manuscript to our departmental secretary in Columbia, Ann Wright.

Columbia, Missouri   Eugene N. Lane

BIBLIOGRAPHY OF WORKS CITED BY ABBREVIATION
OR SHORT TITLE

ABSA   Annual of the British School at Athens, London 1894- .

AEM   Archäologisch-Epigraphische Mitteilungen aus Österreich-Ungarn, Vienna 1877-97.

AJA   American Journal of Archaeology, Princeton etc. 1885- .

AM   Deutsches Archäologisches Institut, Athenische Abteilung, Mitteilungen, Stuttgart etc. 1876- .

Annali   Deutsches Archäologisches Institut, Annali, Rome etc. 1829-85.

Arch. Eph.   Archaiologike Ephemeris, Athens 1837- .

BCH   Bulletin de Correspondance Hellénique, Paris 1877- .

BIAB   Bulletin de l'institut archéologique Bulgare, Sofia 1921- .

Blinkenberg   C. Blinkenberg, *Archäologische Studien*, Copenhagen 1904.

Brambach, *CIRh*   W. Brambach, *Corpus Inscriptionum Rhenanarum*, Eberfeld 1867.

BSAB   Bulletin de la société archéologique Bulgare, Sofia 1910-20.

Bull. Ep.   Bulletin Epigraphique, published in Revue des Etudes Grecques, 1929- .

Bulletino   Deutsches Archäologisches Institut, Bulletino, Rome etc. 1829-85.

Bull. Comun.   Bulletino Archeologico Comunale di Roma, Rome 1872- .

Buresch, *Aus Lydien*   K. Buresch, *Aus Lydien*, Leipzig 1898.

CIG   Corpus Inscriptionum Graecarum, Berlin 1828-77.

CIL   Corpus Inscriptionum Latinarum, Berlin 1862- .

Cook, *Zeus*   A. B. Cook, *Zeus, a Study in Ancient Religion*, Cambridge 1914-40.

CRAI   Académie des Inscriptions et Belles Lettres, Comptes Rendus, Paris 1857- .

Cumont, *Textes et Monuments*   F. Cumont, *Textes et Monuments figurés relatifs aux Mystères de Mithra* I-II, Brussels 1896-1898.

Dessau, *ILS*   H. Dessau, *Inscriptiones Latinae Selectae*, third edition, Berlin 1962.

Dittenberger, *OGIS*   W. Dittenberger, *Orientis Graeci Inscriptiones Selectae*, Leipzig 1903-05.

Herrmann, *Ergebnisse*   P. Herrmann, *Ergebnisse einer Reise in Nordostlydien*, Akademie der Wissenschaften in Wien, Phil.-Hist. Klasse, Denkschriften 80, 1962.

IG   Inscriptiones Graecae, Berlin 1873- .

IGR   R. Cagnat, *Inscriptiones Graecae ad Res Romanas Pertinentes*, Paris 1901-27.

JHS   Journal of Hellenic Studies, London 1880- .

Kalinka, *Antike Denkmäler*   E. Kalinka, *Antike Denkmäler in Bulgarien*, Akademie der Wissenschaften in Wien, Balkankommission, Antiquarische Abteilung, Schriften 4, 1906.

Kazarow, *Beitrag*   G. Kazarow, *Beitrag zur antiken Geschichte von Sofia*, Sofia 1910.

Keil and von Premerstein, *Zweite Reise*   J. Keil and A. von Premerstein, *Bericht über eine zweite Reise in Lydien*, Akademie der Wissenschaften in Wien, Phil.-Hist. Klasse, Denkschriften 54 ii, 1911.

Michel, *Recueil*   C. Michel, *Recueil d'inscriptions grecques*, Paris 1897-1900.

Mihailov, *IGBulg*   G. Mihailov, *Inscriptiones Graecae in Bulgaria Repertae*, Sofia 1956-66.

Mouseion kai Bibliotheke   *Mouseion kai Bibliotheke tes Evangellikes Scholes*, Smyrna 1873-86.

Nilsson, *GGR*   M. P. Nilson, *Geschichte der griechischen Religion*, vol. I, third
                              edition, Munich 1967; vol. II, second edition, Munich 1961.
Öster. Jahreshefte   *Österreichisches Archäologisches Institut, Jahreshefte*, Vienna
                              1898- .
Poxy   The Oxyrrhynchus Papyri, London 1898- .
RA   Revue Archéologique, Paris 1844- .
Ramsay, *Cities and*   W. M. Ramsay, *The Cities and Bishoprics of Phrygia*, Oxford
Bishoprics   1895-97.
RE   Pauly-Wissowa, Real-Encyclopädie der classischen Alter-
                              tumswissenschaft, Stuttgart etc. 1894- .
Sbornik   Bulgarska akademiia na naukite, Sbornik zu narodni umotvoreniia
                              i narodopis, Sofia 1889- .
Steinleitner, *Die Beicht*   F. S. Steinleitner, *Die Beicht im Zusammenhange mit der sakralen
                              Rechtspflege in der Antike*, Diss. Munich 1913.
Sterrett, *Epigraphical*   J. R. S. Sterret, *An Epigraphical Journey in Asia Minor*, Papers of
Journey   the American School of Classical Studies at Athens 2, Boston 1888.
TAM   Tituli Asiae Minoris, Vienna 1901- .
Tacheva-Hitova   Margarita Tacheva-Hitova, "Wesenzüge des Sabazioskultes in
                              Moesia Inferior und Thracia," in *Hommages à Maarten J. Ver-
                              maseren* 3, Etudes préliminaires aux religions orientales dans
                              l'empire romain 68, Leiden 1978, pp. 1217-30.
Tacheva-Hitova,   Margarita Tacheva-Hitova, *Eastern Cults in Moesia Inferior and
Eastern Cults*   Thracia (5th century BC-4th century AD)*, Etudes préliminaires aux
                              religions orientales dans l'empire romain 95, Leiden 1983.
Vermaseren, *CCCA*   M. J. Vermaseren, *Corpus Cultus Cybelae Attidisque*, Etudes
                              préliminaires aux religions orientales dans l'empire romain 50,
                              Leiden 1977- .
Vermaseren, *CIMRM*   M. J. Vermaseren, *Corpus Inscriptionum et Monumentorum
                              Religionis Mithriacae* I-II, The Hague 1956-1960.
Vidman, *SIRIS*   L. Vidman, *Sylloge Inscriptionum Religionis Isiacae et Sarapiacae*,
                              Religionsgeschichtliche Versuche und Vorarbeiten 28, Berlin 1969.
Walters, *Catalogue*   Walters, H. B., *Catalogue of the Bronzes, Greek, Roman and
                              Etruscan, in the Department of Greek and Roman Antiquities,
                              British Museum*, London 1899.
Welles, *Royal*   C. B. Welles, *Royal Correspondence in the Hellenistic period*, New
Correspondence*   Haven 1934.
Ziebarth, *Vereinswesen*   E.G.L. Ziebarth, *Das griechische Vereinswesen*, Leipzig 1896.
ZPE   Zeitschrift für Papyrologie und Epigraphik, Bonn 1967- .

For the complete bibliography, see M. J. Vermaseren, *De onderlinge betrekkingen tussen Mithras-Sabazius-Cybele* in *Academiae Analecta* 46, Brussels 1984, 27-42.

INSCRIBED MONUMENTS,
EXCLUDING INSCRIBED HANDS

THRACIA

Serdica: Sofia

1. A quadrangular altar of limestone, found in October, 1889, in the course of excavating a foundation for the house of Kosta Makedonec in Lom Street, Sofia. Now Sofia Museum, inv. no. 702.

Dimensions: height 0.60; width 0.57; thickness 0.52 to 0.70; letters 0.035 to 0.045.

> *AEM* 14, 1891, p. 150 no. 25; Kalinka, *Antike Denkmäler*, col. 166 no. 185; Dobrusky, *Sbornik* 2, 1890, p. 4f. no. 2; Kazarow, *Beitrag*, p. 80 no. 20; Mihailov, *IG Bulg* IV, 1927; Tacheva-Hitova, no. 7; Tacheva-Hitova, *Eastern Cults*, no. III 8.

Inscription:　　['Αγαθη Τύχη]
　　　　　　　　κυρίῳ Σαβαζ[ί]ῳ
　　　　　　　　'Αθυπαρηνῷ
　　　　　　　　Αὐρ. Διζᾶς Λουκίου
　　　　　5　　ἱερεὺς ἀνέστησεν
　　　　　　　　ἐκξ εὐχῆς τὸν ναόν.

Buhovo, in area of ancient **Serdica**

2. A limestone altar, known since before 1901, now in Sofia Museum, inv. no. 2870.

Dimensions: height 1.00; width 0.57; thickness 0.54; letters 0.030 to 0.035.

> Dobrusky, *Sbornik* 18, 1901, p. 782-3 no. 93; *IGR* I, no. 679; Weinreich, *AM* 37, 1912, p. 17 no. 78; Kazarow, *Beitrag*, p. 88 no. 70; Mihailov, *IG Bulg* IV, 1985; Tacheva-Hitova, no. 8; Tacheva-Hitova, *Eastern Cults*, no. III 9.

Inscription:　　'Αγαθη Τύχη
　　　　　　　　ἐπηκόῳ θεῷ
　　　　　　　　Σεβαζίῳ Μητρι-
　　　　　　　　κῷ Αὐρ. 'Αστικὸς
　　　　　　　　Φειλίου βοηθὸς
　　　　　5　　κορνικουλαρί[ων]
　　　　　　　　εὐξάμενος ἀνέστησ(εν)
　　　　　　　　εὐτυχῶς.

Mramor, in area of ancient **Serdica**

3. A limestone altar, broken on top and on right, known since before 1910. Now Sofia Museum, inv. no. 2958.
Dimensions: height 0.90; width 0.35; thickness 0.39.

> Kazarow, *Beitrag*, p. 89 no. 72; Mihailov, *IG Bulg* IV, 2015; Tacheva-Hitova, no. 9; Tacheva-Hitova, *Eastern Cults*, no. III 10.

Inscription: Διὶ Σεβαζίωι ὁ ἱερε[ὺς....]
                 Μόκας Δίζου ΤΩΝΕΚ[......]
                 κατεσκεύασεν καὶ ΔΟ[....]
                 ΜΑΙ ΩΝΙΩΙΛΑ
                       vacat
            5   [......]αλος ἐποίει
                 [Μ]ο[υ]χαλᾶς Οἰμήδου
                 leaf ΝΙΕΙ leaf
                 [.....]Τάρσας 'Ροίμου
                 [.....]χενθου Μόκα

Maslovo, in area of ancient **Serdica**

4. A limestone altar, broken down the middle into two pieces. Found before 1961 on the left bank of the river Blato, 25 to 30 meters to the right of the bridge at the town market-place. Now Sofia Museum, inv. no. 8113.
Dimensions: height 1.13; width 0.57; thickness 0.57; letters 0.030 to 0.035.

> T. Ivanov, *Arkheologija* 3, 1961, fasc. 4, p. 40-43 and fig. 1-2; Mihailov, *IG Bulg* IV, 2023; Tacheva-Hitova, no. 10; Tacheva-Hitova, *Eastern Cults*, no. III 11.

Inscription: Σεβαζίῳ ἐπηκόῳ
                 Π(όπλιος) Αἴλ(ιος) 'Ιουλιανὸς
                 στρατευσάμενος ἐν
                 πρετωρίῳ θεοῦ Μ(άρκου) Αὐρ(ηλίου)
            5   'Αντωνίνου Σευήρου
                 ἐκ τῶν εἰδίων κατε-
                 σκεύασεν τὸ ἔργον ὑ-
                 πὲρ ἑαυτοῦ κὲ τῶν ἀ-
                 δελφῶν Αἰ(λίων) Μάρχου
           10   κὲ 'Ηρακλίδου.

Julianus was pretorian between 198 and 217.

Dragoman, in area of ancient **Serdica**

5. A plaque first seen before 1886 by a Serbian officer at the entrance of the church of St. Peter on the hill called Dragomanski-Tepnik. Now in Sofia Museum, inv. no. 1231.

Dimensions: height 0.175; width 0.29 at top, 0.49 at bottom; letters 0.02.

A von Domaszewski, *AEM* 10, 1886, p. 239 no. 3; Kalinka, *Antike Denkmäler*, col. 165 no. 184; Kazarow, *Beitrag*, p. 89 no. 71; *IGR* I, 678; Mihailov, *IG Bulg* IV, 2034; Tacheva-Hitova, no. 11; Tacheva-Hitova, *Eastern Cults*, no. III 12.

Inscription: Ἀγαθῆι Τύ(χηι) Αὐρ. Μεστρια[νὸς]
                 στρατ(ιώτης) λεγ(ιῶνος) β΄ Πα[ρθικῆς]
                 κυρίῳ Σαβαζίῳ ἐ[κ]
                 προνοίας εὐχαρισ[τή-]
              5 ριον ἔστησεν.

After 197 A.D.

Pirot, in the territory of **Serdica**
(now on Jugoslav side of frontier)

6.   An altar of limestone, first seen by A. von Domaszewski before 1886. Apparently never taken to a museum.

Dimensions: height 0.81; width 0.60; thickness 0.40.

AEM 10, 1886, p. 258 no. 2; Sofija Kojić, *Starinar* (N.S.) 15-16, 1964-1965, pp. 183-186; Tacheva-Hitova, pp. 1218-19, with doubts as to correctness of restoration.

Inscription: Ἀγαθη [Τύ]χ[η]
                 θεῷ ἐπηκόῳ ὑψίστῳ
                 εὐχὴν ἀνέστησαν
                 τὸ κοινὸν ἐκ τῶν ἰ-
              5 δίων διὰ ἱερέως
                 Ἑρμογένους καὶ προ-
                 στάτου Αὐγουστιανοῦ
                 Ἀχιλλεύς, Αὐρῆλις, Δῖο(ς), Ἀλέ-
                 ξανδρος, Μόκας, Μο[κι]ανός,
             10 Δομῆτις, Σοφεῖνος, Παυ-
                 λεῖνος, Πόρος, Ἀπολινά-
                 ρις, Μοχιανός, [Σ]ῆλος
                 καὶ Ἀλέξανδρος Ἀσχ-
                 ληκιάδου, θία[σος] Σεβαζι-
             15 ανὸς ΘΗ....ΤΟΥΤΑΣ

Taurisana?: Tavalićevo

7.   An altar of course stone, found at a place called Grobo in the village of Tavaličevo before 1906. Subsequently taken to the Sofia Museum, where it was given the inv. no. 3398, but later lost.

Dimensions: height 0.80; length 0.60; thickness 0.40.

Mihailov, *IG Bulg* IV, 2196, with references to earlier bibliography, all inaccessible to me; Tacheva-Hitova, no. 4; Tacheva-Hitova, *Eastern Cults*, no. III 15.

Inscription: Κυρίῳ Σεβαζ[ίῳ]
ἐπηκ[ό]ῳ Μᾶρ(κ)[ος]
Μου[κα]κέρζ[ου]
[κ]αὶ ....ΟΥ...
5 .ΕΟΘΙ καὶ Μ[ᾶρ-]
κο(ς) Βελίου [εὐξά-]
[μ]ενοι τὸ[ν βωμὸν]
[ἀνέθηκαν.]

Pautalia: Kyustendil

8. A fragment of marble, preserved only on the right, known since 1952. It was transported to the Kyustendil Museum, and subsequently lost. Dimensions: height 0.88; width 0.375; letters 0.030 to 0.038.

V. Beseliev, *Epigrafski Prinosi* (1952), p. 64-5; Mihailov, *IG Bulg* IV, 2103; Tacheva-Hitova, no. 13; Tacheva-Hitova, *Eastern Cults*, no. III. 14.

Inscription: ᾿Αγαθῇ Τύχῃ
(Διὶ) Σεβαζίωι
ΙΝ..Σ..ΒΕ
. ΚΤΑΛΙΝ
5 ...ΤΥΟΕΠΙ
...ΝΕΟΣ
...ΕΟΣ

9. An altar of syenite stone, with acroteria, found before 1919 on the hill called Hisarlaka, now housed in a hotel on the same hill. Dimensions: height 0.80; width 0.50; thickness 0.50; lettes 0.03 to 0.04.

J. Ivanov, *BSAB* 7, 1919-20, p. 83 no. 3 and fig. 53; *SEG* I, 302; Mihailov, *IG Bulg* IV, 2076, with additional bibliography; Tacheva-Hitova, no. 12; Tacheva-Hitova, *Eastern Cults*, no. III 13.

Inscription: ᾿Αγαθῇ Τύχῃ
Διὶ Σεβαζίῳ
Χρῆστος Ζωίλου.

**Kespetli (Karanovo), apparently
transported from Augusta Traiana (Beroea): Stara Zagora**

10. Two joining fragments of marble, now in Sofia Museum, inv. no. 395 and 396. First seen by Dobrusky before 1895.

Dimensions: a) height 0.45; length 0.70; thickness 0.26. b) height 0.40; length 0.65; thickness 0.28.

V. Dobrusky, *AEM*, 18, 1895, p. 119 no. 36; *Sbornik* 12, 1895, p. 334 no. 25; *IGR* I, 744; Mihailov, *IG Bulg* III ii, 1588; Tacheva-Hitova, no. 19; Tacheva-Hitova, *Eastern Cults*, no. III 21.

Inscription: Ἀγαθῆι Τύχ[ηι]
ἐπὶ αὐτοκράτορος Λ. Σεπτιμίου Σεουήρου [Σεβαστοῦ καὶ Μ. Αὐρ.
Ἀντω-]
νίνου Καίσαρος ὑπάτων Διὶ Σεβαζίωι Ἀρσε[ληνῷ τὸν ναὸν]
κατασκευασθέντα ἐπὶ βασιλέως Θρ[ακῶν ....καὶ ὑ-]
5 πὸ τοῦ μακροῦ χρ[όνο]υ διαφθαρέντ[α....................]

202 A.D., but recording restoration of earlier temple.

Javorovo, in area
of **Augusta Traiana (Beroea)**

11. A fragmentary tablet of marble, known since 1965, now in Stara Zagora Museum.

Dimensions: height 0.45; length 0.94; thickness 0.34; letters 0.035 to 0.038.

Buyukliev, *Arkheologija* 7, 1965, fasc. 2, p. 50-51 and fig. 1; Tacheva-Hitova, no. 18; Tacheva-Hitova, *Eastern Cults*, no. III 20; G. Mihailov, *Epigraphica* 37, 1975, p. 50-51.

Inscription: Τὸ ιε΄ Διὶ Σαβαζίῳ θεῷ προγονικῶι
Τίτος Φλαούιος Σκέλου υἱὸς Κυρείνα Δί-
νις ἱερεὺς ἀπὸ προγόνων διὰ βίου καὶ
5 ἀρχιερεὺς τοῦ κοινοῦ τῆς ἐπαρχείας
τὸν βωμὸν ἐκ τῶν ἰδίων κατεσκεύασεν.

The editor wishes to date this inscription to the reign of Vespasian, something which would make it the second-earliest of Zeus-Sabazius identification (after no. 27, below), but Mihailov points out that the letter-forms allow a date as late as the Antonine period.

Sportela: Rila

12. A plaque of syenite, known since ca. 1926. Seen first in the house of Peter Zlatanov, where the right part is still preserved, but supposed to have been brought from a chapel of St. George, on hill to west of town.

Dimensions: height 0.64; length 1.65; thickness 0.32; letters 0.04 to 0.05. The preserved portion has a length of 0.91.

Velkov, *BIAB* 4, 1926-27, p. 319; Mihailov, *IG Bulg* IV, 2233; Tacheva-Hitova, no. 15; Tacheva-Hitova, *Eastern Cults*, no. III 16.

Inscription: Ἀγαθῆι Τύχηι
Κυρίῳ Σαβαζίῳ κληρονόμοι Πιξισείσου Αἰσυ-
μώους καὶ ἀδελφῶν αὐτοῦ Σπορτηληνοὶ ἐποί-
ησαν ἐκ τῶν ἐκείνου δι' ἐπιμελητῶν Βείθυος
5 Μουκατράλεος καὶ Λούππου Πι[εισ]είσου καὶ Μάρ-
κου καὶ Λουκίου.

MOESIA SUPERIOR

Timacum Minus: Ravna

13. A limestone altar, apparently discovered subsequent to 1941, and taken to the museum of Niš, where it could not be found in 1966. Possibly destroyed in 1944 bombardment.
Dimensions: height 1.10; width 0.45; thickness 0.45.

N. Vulić, *Spomenik Srpske akademije nauka* 98, 1941-8, p. 82 no. 173; L. Zotović *Les Cultes orientaux sur le territoire de la Mésie Supérieure*, EPRO 7, Leiden 1966, p. 104-5, no. 50.

Inscription: Pro salute imp(eratoris)
Flaviu[s] Cleme[s]
Saba[zi]o pate -
rno v(otum) l(ibens) posu-
5 i[t M. Ant]o[nio]
G[o]rdiano
Aug. [et]
[P]omp(eiano) [c]oss.

241 A.D.

MOESIA INFERIOR

Municipium Montanensium; Kutlovica (Mikhailovgrad)

14. A limestone altar, now lost.
Dimensions: height 1.07; width 0.42; thickness 0.28.

Domaszewski, *CIL* III, 7448; L. Vidman, *SIRIS* 701 (both with attribution to Sarapis); Dobrusky, *Sbornik* 16-17, 1900, p. 79 (correcting the reading); Tacheva-Hitova, no. 1; Tacheva-Hitova, *Eastern Cults*, no. III 1.

Inscription: Numini Sabazio Cessicius
[......Iu]lianus ex vo-
to posuit.

Pavlikeni, in area of **Nicopolis ad Istrum**

15. A limestone base, first seen by H. and K. Skorpil before 1892 on the farm of Atanas Slavchev. Now in Pavlikeni public garden.
Dimensions: height ca. 1.00; width 0.44; thickness 0.41.

> *AEM* 15, 1892, p. 210 no. 84; *CIL* III, 12429; G. Seure, *RA* 1908 II, p. 43 no. 43; Tacheva-Hitova no. 4; Tacheva-Hitova, *Eastern Cults*, no. III 5.

Inscription: Iov[i]
Saba-
dio
et Mercur[i]o
5 M. S[e]rvili-
us Verecun-
dus pro se e[t] suos
votum posuit
[l(ibens)] m(erito).

Nicopolis ad Istrum: Nikyup

16. An altar, first seen by A. von Domaszewski before 1886, still built into a wall belonging to A. G. Popov.
Dimensions: height 0.50; width 0.38; letters 0.045 in first line, 0.030 to 0.035 elsewhere.

> Domaszewski, *AEM* 10, 1886, p. 241 no. 6; G. Seure, *RA* 1908 II, p. 44 no. 45; Mihailov, *IG Bulg* II, 678, with further bibliographical references; Tacheva-Hitova, no. 3; Tacheva-Hitova, *Eastern Cults*, no. III 4.

Inscription: [Θεᾶς] Ἰδείας μεγάλης
[καὶ τ]οῦ Διὶ Ἡλίῳ μεγά[λῳ]
[κυρί]ῳ Σεβαζίῳ Ἀ[ρσι-]
[λη]νῷ Φλ. Ἀσια[νὸς]
5 [......]ου βουλ(ευτὴς) ὑπ[ὲρ τῆς]
[ἑαυτ]οῦ σωτηρ[ίας τὸ]
[εὐχα]ρ[ι]στ[ήριον]
[ἀνέστησεν.]

17. An altar of limestone, see first by Dobrusky before 1900. Now in Sofia Museum, inv. no. 2258.
Dimensions: height 1.00; width 0.48; thickness 0.46; depression in top 0.20 depth, 0.20 diameter; channel for libations, 0.035 length.

> Dobrusky, *Sbornik* 16-17, 1900, p. 79; G. Seure, *RA* 1908 II, p. 43-4 no. 44; Weinreich, *AM* 37, 1912, p. 18, no. 79; Mihailov, *IG Bulg* II, 677, with further bibliographical references; Tacheva-Hitova, no. 2; Tacheva-Hitova, *Eastern Cults*, no. III 3.

Inscription: Ἀγαθῇ Τύχῃ
                 Μουκάζενις Αὐλου-
                 κένθου θεῷ ἐπη-
                 κόῳ Σαβαζίῳ Ἀρ-
        5   σιληνῷ ὑπὲρ ἑαυτοῦ.

Turgovishte (Vishovgrad), in area of Nicopolis ad Istrum

18.   A limestone altar, of which only the top part is preserved, known since
before 1907. Now in the Sofia Museum, inv. no. 3913.
Dimensions unavailable.

> Dobrusky, *Sbornik* 22-23, 1907, p. 172 no. 210 (*non vidi*); *Année Epigraphique* 1908,
> no. 141; Tacheva-Hitova no. 5; Tacheva-Hitova, *Eastern Cults*, no. III 6.

Inscription: Iovi Sabadio
                 et Mercurio
                 M. E(nnius?) Celerinus
                 pro se et suis
        5   v(otum) s(olvit).

DACIA SUPERIOR

Potaissa: Turda

19.   A fragmentary altar of limestone conglomerate, found in 1948 at no. 3
Traian St., in the course of demolishing a house damaged in a 1944 bombardment. The stone was probably brought to the house as building material
in the 19th century. It is now in the Turda museum.
Dimensions: height 0.37; width 0.25; thickness 0.18; letters 0.03.

> I. I. Russu, *Din activitatea muzeelor noastre* I, Cluj 1955, p. 102 f.; M. Macrea, *Dacia*
> (N.S.) 3, 1959, p. 327; *Année Epigraphique* 1956, no. 267; *Apulum* 4, 1961, p. 87.

Inscription: Iovi S-
                 abazi-
                 o [A]ur.
                 [Marcel-]
        5   [lin]us
                 traces of letters

Apulum: Alba Iulia

20.   A votive plaque of limestone, preserved only on right. It was
discovered by chance in 1912, and now is in the Alba Iulia Museum, inv. no.
159/1/.

Dimensions: height 0.40; width 0.34; thickness 0.058, height of field 0.25; letters 0.028 to 0.033.

M. Macrea, *Dacia* (N.S.) 3, 1959, pp. 325-7; *Apulum* 4, 1961, p. 65.

Inscription: [Iovi S]abasio
               [pro sal. I]mp. Caes.
               [M. Aur. Ant]onini pii fel(icis)
               [Aug. et Iuliae] Aug(ustae) matris
        5 [Aug. a deo i]ussus fecit
               [L. Aurel. M]arcianus
               [aedil]icius.

Reign of Caracalla, 211-218 A.D.

PROVINCIAE ASIAE MINORIS

Karamanlı Camii, in ancient **Bithynia**

21. A basis, previously adorned with a relief, built into the wall of a mosque. It was first seen by F. K. Dörner before 1941, in a cemetery S. W. of Işakcılar.

Dimensions: height 1.14; width 0.45 at the top, 0.42 at the inscription field, and 0.565 at the bottom; letters 0.03 in line 1, 0.027 elsewhere.

F. K. Dörner, *Inschriften und Denkmäler aus Bithynien*, Istanbuler Forschungen 14, Berlin 1941, p. 62 no. 35 and Pl. 22.

Inscription: Διὶ Σαβαζίῳ
               Διόδωρος Διοδώρου
               τοῦ Διοδώρου κα-
               τὰ εὐχὴν ἀνέθηκεν
        5 ἔτους γ΄ Ἀδριανοῦ Καίσα-
               ρος Πριετήου δ.΄

27 May, 119 A.D.

Işakcılar (Sakcılar), in ancient **Bithynia**

22. A basis of limestone, reused as a column base, inscribed on all sides and now built into the railing on the way up to the mosque. Apparently there were once reliefs under the inscriptions. It was first seen by F. K. Dörner before 1941.

Dimensions: height 0.51; width 0.38; thickness 0.40; letters 0.030 to 0.035.

F. K. Dörner, *op. cit.*, p. 62 no. 34 and Pl. 21.

Inscription: Σεῖος Ζαρδοήλου

Δὶ Σαβαζίῳ κατ᾽ ὁ-
νίρου ἐπιταγὴν
ἐποῖσε
5 οἰκῶν ἐν φυ-
λῇ Πετροζέ-
τοις
ἔτους δευτέρου
Νέρουα Τρα-
10 ειανοῦ Κέσα-
ρος
Τειμοκράτης
Μοκάζιος ἐποί-
ησε.

99 A.D.

Dacibyza: Gebseh, near **Nicomedeia**

23.   A marble altar, in front of local mosque in 1976. It was first seen by
Belsen in 1762, and most recently by S. Şahin and E. Schwertheim in 1976.
The reading has been considerably disputed over the years, but that of Şahin
and Schwertheim is followed here.

Dimensions: height undeterminable, as part is buried; width 0.65;
thickness 0.55; letters 0.035.

> *CIG*, 3791; Henzen, *Bulletino*, 1848; p. 82-83; Keil, *Philologus* 7, 1852, p. 201;
> Koerte, *AM* 24, 1899, p. 425 no. 21; Siderides, *Hellenikos Philologikos Syllogos en
> Konstantinoupolei* 27, 1895-99, p. 284 no. 5; Dörner, *op. cit.*, p. 40f. and *RE*, 18 ii,
> cols. 679 and 2588; Robert, *Hellenica* 7, 1949, p. 45 f. and 10, 1955, Pl. VI, 3; Şahin
> and Schwertheim, *ZPE* 24, 1977, p. 260f.; *TAM* IV i, no. 79.

Inscription: Ἀγαθῇ Τύχῃ
Θεῷ Σαβαζίῳ Παγισα-
ρανῷ τὸν βωμὸν ἀνέ-
στησα Μάξιμος Μου-
5 κιανοῦ εὐχαριστήριον
ἔτους θ΄ Σεουήρου καὶ
Ἀντωνίνου Σεβαστῶν.

206 A.D.

After I finished the manuscript, the following further discussion of this inscription came to my attention. In *BCH* 102, 1978, p. 432-437, Louis Robert
again passes in review the various readings which have been made of this
document, and publishes new photographs. He concludes that the correct
reading should be Πατισαρανῷ. The matter is again reviewed in *SEG* 27 (1977),

no. 825, with refusal to judge between the reading of Şahin-Schwertheim and that of Robert. As Robert remarks, it does not make much difference in the present state of our knowledge, as the epithet is of unknown origin and unattested elsewhere.

See also now, *Die Inschriften von Kalchedon*, Inschriften griechischer Städte aus Kleinasien 20, Bonn 1980, no. 103.

Syllanta (?): Keskin, near Gölpazarı, Turkey

24. An altar of limestone, built into the village fountain. It is said to have come from a spot called Türbe Deresi, about 2 km. N.E. of the village. Dimensions: height 0.77; width 0.35; letters 0.03.

> S. Sahin, *Katalog der antiken Inschriften des Museums von Iznik (Nikaia)* II, i, Inschriften griechischer Städte aus Kleinasien 10, i, Bonn 1981, no. 1127.

Inscription: Διὶ Σαουαζίῳ
              καὶ δήμῳ Συλλαν-
              τηνῶν
              ἔτους ϛ´ Ἁδρι-
          5   ανοῦ Καίσαρ-
              ος Σεβαστοῦ.

122-3 A.D.

Blaudos?: Balat?

25. A stele showing an incense-offering to Zeus-Sabazius. On the left, Zeus-Sabazius is seated on a throne and holds a spear and a patera. In the middle, there is an altar, and behind it a snake wraps itself around a tree. On the right, there is one male and one female worshipper; the man appears to be putting incense on the altar. The inscription is under the relief. The stone was first seen by Conze in 1857 on Imbros. It was said to be from Balat, between Prusa and Pergamum. It now appears to be lost. Dimensions: height 0.25; width 0.18.

> Conze, *Reise auf den Inseln des thrakischen Meeres*, p. 98 f and Pl. 17 no. 7; Keil, *Philologus* Suppl. 2, 1893, p. 606; Cook, *Zeus*, 2 i, p. 183.

Inscription: Μένανδρος Ἀθηνοδώ-
              ρου Διὶ Σααζίῳ
              εὐχήν.

Pergamum: Bergama

26. A small marble column with profiled base, a dowel-hole for a votive gift at the top. It was found in the excavations of 1906 in front of the Auditorium, and is now in the Pergamum excavation-house.

Dimensions: height 0.12; height of letters 0.012 to 0.013; interlineation 0.001.

P. Jacobsthal, *AM* 33, 1908, p. 402 f. no. 29. Discussion in E. Ohlemutz, *Die Kulte und Heilgtümer der Götter in Pergamon*, Darmstadt 1968, p. 269-272, concerning this and the following inscription.

Inscription: Σαβαζίω
          [Φ]ιλωτέρα Ἀμυνίου
          κατ' ἐπιταγήν.

27.   A stele of white marble, mutilated above and broken in two parts. The parts were found in the North Portico of the Temple of Athena in December 1880 and May 1883, respectively. It is now housed in the Staatliche Museen of East Berlin, Antikensammlung, inv. no. 248.

Dimensions: width at top 0.440, at bottom 0.485; thickness 0.085; letters 0.008; height incomplete.

Conze, *Berlin Akademie Monatsberichte*, 1881, p. 869 and Pl. IV; M. Fränkel, *Altertümer von Pergamon*, 8 i, p. 164 no. 248 and Addenda, 8 ii, p. 510; Michel, *Recueil*, p. 59 no. 46; Dittenberger, *OGIS*, p. 509 no. 331; Welles, *Royal Correspondence*, nos. 65-66.

Inscription (only relevant portion given):

45 Βασιλεὺς Ἄτταλος Περγαμηνῶν τῆι βουλῆι καὶ τῶι δήμωι χαίρειν· ἐπεὶ βασ[ί]-
   λισσα Στρατονίκη ἡ μήτηρ μου εὐσεβεστάτη μὲγ γενομένη πασῶν, φιλ[ο]-
   στοργοτάτη δὲ διαφερόντως πρός τε τὸμ πατέρα μου καὶ πρὸς ἐμέ,
   πρὸς ἄπαντας μὲν τοὺς θεοὺς εὐσεβῶς προσηνέχθη, μάλιστα δὲ
   πρὸς τὸν Δία τὸν Σαβάζιον, πατροπαράδοτον αὐτὸγ κομίσασα εἰς
50 τὴμ πατρίδα ἡμῶν, ὄγ καὶ ἐμ πολλαῖς πράξεσι καὶ ἐμ πολλοῖς κινδύ-
   νοις παραστάτηγ καὶ βοηθὸν ἡμῖγ γενόμενον ἐκρίναμεν διὰ τὰς ἐξ αὐτοῦ
   γενομένας ἐπιφανείας συγκαθιερῶσαι τῆι Νικηφόρωι Ἀθηνᾶι, νομίσαν-
   τες τοῦτον αὐτῶι ἄξιον καὶ πρέποντα τόπον ὑπάρχειν, διεταξάμε-
   θα δὲ ἀκολούθως τούτοις καὶ περὶ θυσιῶγ καὶ πομπῶγ καὶ μυστηρίων
55 τῶν ἐπιτελουμένωμ πρὸ πόλεως αὐτῶι ἐν τοῖς καθήκουσι καιροῖς καὶ τόποις.
   ἐποήσαμεν δὲ αὐτοῦ καὶ ἱερέα διὰ γένους Ἀθήναιον τὸν ἐμόν, εὐσεβείαι κα[ὶ]
   καλοκἀγαθίαι διαφέροντα καὶ τῆι πρὸς ἡμᾶς πίστει κρίνομεν διὰ ταῦ- -
   τα, ὅπως ἂν εἰς τὸν ἄπαντα χρόνον ἀκίνητα καὶ ἀμετάθετα μένηι τά τε πρὸς
   τὸν θεὸν τίμια καὶ τὰ πρὸς τὸν Ἀθήναιομ φιλάνθρωπα, τὰ γραφέντα ὑφ' ἡμῶμ
60 προστάγματα ἐν τοῖς ἱεροῖς νόμοις φέρεσθαι παρ' ὑμῖν.
   δ΄, Δίου δ΄, Λύτος ἐκ Περγάμου.

135-4 B.C.

Teos: Sivrihissar

28.   A grave stele of white marble, broken all around. Above, there is an ornament like a crown. First seen by R. Demangel and A. Laumonier in the fall of 1921, built into a fountain S.E. of city.

Dimensions: height 0.80*; width 0.31; letters 0.03.

BCH 46, 1922, p. 341 no. 30; SEG, II, 608.

Inscription: [E]ὐβούλα Μηνοφίλου
                    Ἀθηναία χαῖρε
                    οἱ Σαβαζιασταί.

* The publication gives 0.08, but this is clearly impossible.

Ephesus: Selcuk

29. A small altar of white marble, with a dowel-hole in the bottom, a shallow depression in the top. The letters are badly scribbled. Found in 1900 in the Austrian excavations in the Harbor Street near the four column-bases, built into a late wall. Copied by Rudolf Heberdey. Now in excavation house, inv. no. 733.

Dimensions: height 0.21; width 0.175; thickness 0.17; letters 0.01 to 0.0125.

J. Keil, Öster.Jahreshefte 35, 1940 Beiblatt, col. 108; L. Robert, Bull. Ep. 1944, no. 161a; H. Engelmann - D. Knibbe, Öster.Jahreshefte 52, 1978-1980, 48 no. 87 [1242]; L. Robert, Bull. Ep. 1981, no. 426; Inschriften von Ephesos IV, Inschriften griechischer Städte aus Kleinasien 14, Bonn 1980, 141-142 no. 1242.

Inscription: Διὶ
                    Σαβαζίῳ

Sardis: Sart

30. A fragment of a marble slab, found in the course of the American Excavations of 1958. Now preserved in excavation house.

Dimensions: height 0.47; width 0.32; thickness 0.15; letters of first five lines 0.015 to 0.025, of sixth 0.035 to 0.040.

Sherman E. Johnson, Religions in Antiquity, Studies in the History of Religions 14, 1968, p. 542-550.

Inscription (restorations quite uncertain):

               [Μη]νόφιλος Μηνο[φίλου]
               [φυλ]ῆς Εὐμενηΐδος ἱε[ρεὺς]
               [Διὸς] Σαυαζίου ἐν τῶι ν[αῶι]
               [φυ]λῆι Εὐμενηΐδι τὸν βω[μὸν]
          5   Διὶ
               [x]αὶ Θεᾷ Σ[.............]

Apparently of the reign of Eumenes II, 197-159 B.C.

31. A block of marble, found in late June 1974 reused in a late-Roman bath building. Now preserved in the excavation house.
Dimensions: height 0.455; width 0.585.

L. Robert, *CRAI*, 1975, p. 306-330; Sokolowski, *ZPE* 34, 1979, p. 65f.

Inscription: Ἐτέων τριήκοντα ἐννέα Ἀρτα-
ξέρξεω βασιλεύοντος, τὸν ἀν-
δριάντα Δροαφέρνης vac.
Βαρακέω Λυδίης ὕπαρχος Βαρα-
5 δατέῳ Διί. leaf Προστάσσει τοῖς
εἰσπορευομένοις εἰς τὸ ἄδυ-
τον νεωκόροις θεραπευ-
ταῖς αὐτοῦ καὶ στεφανοῦσι τὸν θεὸν μὴ μετέχειν μυστηρίων Σαβα-
10 ζίου τῶν τὰ ἔνπυρα βασταζόν-
των καὶ Ἀνγδίστεως καὶ Μᾶς. Προσ-
τάσσουσι δὲ Δοράτῃ τῷ νεωκόρῳ τούτων τῶν μυστηρίων ἀπέχεσθαι.

Apparently a second-century A.D. reinscription of an inscription from the time of Artaxerxes II.

Sandal

32. A low three-stepped block of marble, probably a basis, with the inscription on the front of the top step. First seen before 1880, and apparently again by Buresch before 1898. The dimensions are unknown.

Mouseion kai Bibliotheke, 1880, p. 171 no. tmz'; Buresch, *Aus Lydien*, p. 78; Keil and von Premerstein, *Zweite Reise*, p. 84; *TAM*, V, 1, 594.

Inscription: Κλάδος Μαχάτου ἀπελεύθερος
ὑπὲρ Μαχάτου τῆς σωτηρίας Διὶ Σαβαζίῳ εὐχήν.

33. A stele, with an almost completely obliterated representation of the god's holy grove. Seen first before 1880, and apparently again by Keil and von Premerstein at the time of their second journey. The dimensions are unknown.

Mouseion kai Bibliotheke, 1880, p. 164 no. tlb'; Buresch, *Aus Lydien*, p. 111 bottom; Steinleitner, *Die Beicht*, p. 43 no. 14 with listing of preceding bibliography; Reinach, *RA*, 1885 II, p. 107; Ramsay, *JHS* 8, 1887, p. 227 no. 2; Buckler, *ABSA* 21, 1914-16, p. 170; Keil and von Premerstein, *Zweite Reise*, p. 84; *TAM*, V, 1, 592.

Inscription: Ἔτους τχ, μη(νὸς) Περειτίου ιβ, Αὐρ.
Στρατόνεικος β, ἐπειδὴ κατὰ

ἄγνοιαν ἐκ τοῦ ἄλσου ἔκοψα
δένδρα θεῶν Διὸς Σαβαζίου καὶ
5 Ἀρτέμιδος Ἀνάειτις, κολασθεὶς εὐξάμενος εὐχαριστή-
ριον ἀνέστησα.

235-6 A.D.

34. A stele broken on the right, first seen before 1880. The dimensions are unknown.

> *Mouseion kai Bibliotheke*, 1880, p. 164 no. tlg'; Ramsay, *JHS* 10, 1889, p. 225 no. 17; Steinleitner, *Die Beicht*, p. 43-44 no. 15; Keil and von Premerstein, *Zweite Reise*, p. 84; *TAM* V, 1, 593.

Inscription: Ἔτους [....]ε, μη(νὸς) [Αὐ-]
δναίου ιβ΄ Τρό[φι-]
μος Νεικία ἱε[ρό-]
δουλος, ἐπιζ[ητή-]
5 σαντος Διὸς Σ[αβ-]
αζίου διὰ τὸ κ[ολά-]
ζεσθε αὐτὸν [ἔγρα-]
ψα καὶ ἀνέσσ[τησα]
[τὴν] στήλλην.

Saittae: Üşümüs

35. A fragment of a stele of bluish marble, preserved only on the left, first seen by Keil and von Premerstein in 1908.
Dimensions: height 0.23; width 0.14; thickness 0.075.

> Keil and von Premerstein, *Zweite Reise*, p. 113 no. 218; *TAM*, V, 1, 145.

Inscription: Ἔτους τ[....μη(νὸς)....]
η΄ ἀ(πιόντος) Ἐλιαν[ὸς..]
σιάλου [...............]
κτος εἰσρ[.............]
Σαβαζίῳ [εὐχήν].

After 300 Sullan Era.

Ayazviran, near **Kula**

36. The lower part of a stele of white marble, first seen by P. Herrman in 1961.
Dimensions: height 0.24; width 0.28; thickness 0.06; letters 0.018.

> Hermann, *Ergebnisse*, p. 50-51 no. 45; Robert, *Bull. Ep.* 1963, no. 228; *TAM*, V, 1, 459.

Inscription: traces of letters
ἱερόδουλον Τρόφιμ[ον Μη-]
τρὸς Ἴπτα καὶ Διὸς Σαβαζίου
ποιήσας συρῆναι ὑπὸ ἐξου-
σίας κολασθεὶς ἰς τοὺς ὀφθαλ-
5 μοὺς ἀνέστησε τὴν στήλην.

Koloida (Kollyda): Gyölde

37. A pedimental stele, broken at the bottom. In the main field there are two shovel-like objects in relief, and below them the inscription. First seen before 1880, it was seen again by Keil and von Premerstein at the time of their second journey. They interpret the objects as "kleine, bei den Mysterien verwendete Schaufeln oder Lärminstrumente." The objects are similar to others on some of the votive hands dedicated to Sabazius.

Dimensions: height 0.39; width at top 0.27, at bottom 0.31; thickness (minimum) 0.04.

Mouseion kai Bibliotheke, 1878-80, p. 169 no. tmb'; Keil and von Premerstein, Zweite Reise, p. 96-97 no. 188; TAM, V, 1, 352.

Inscription: Μητρὶ Ἴπτα Διεὶ Σα
[βαζίῳ ....]

37a. Fragment of marble, broken on all sides. First seen by W. M. Ramsay in Gyölde in 1884.
Dimensions: unknown

TAM, V, 1, 356.

Inscription: Σ]αβαζίῳ
]ς Ἰουλ[ι-
]υν[

37b. Fragment of marble, broken on all sides. Above the inscription are preserved the forefeet of a horse. First seen by W. M. Ramsay in Gyölde in 1884.
Dimensions: unknown

TAM, V, 1, 357.

Inscription: Σαβα]ζίῳ Με[
]'Αθηνα[

Maionia: Menye

38. A stele with writing in quadrangular field. Over it, a wreath and ribbon. It was first seen by Keil and von Premerstein in 1908.

Dimensions: height 0.63; width at bottom 0.465; thickness 0.09; letters 0.011 to 0.016.

Keil and von Premerstein, *Zweite Reise*, p. 83-85 no. 168; *TAM*, V, 1, 539.

Inscription: Ἡρακλείδης Ἑρμογένου Γενναίου
                 Διὶ Σαβαζίωι εὐχ[ή]ν.

The *b* of Sabazius and the name of the grandfather were added after the rest of the inscription.

39.   A stele with a representation of a man making a libation at an altar, over which there is a snake. In his left hand the man holds a larger vessel of some kind. The stele has a moulding above and a lug below. It is now in the Manisa Museum, inv. no. 124 5. It has been known since 1961.

Dimensions: height 0.57; width 0.225 to 0.26; thickness 0.075; letters 0.018; interlineation 0.012.

P. Herrmann and K. Z. Polatkan, *Österreichische Akademie der Wissenschaften, Phil.-Hist. Klasse, Anzeiger* 98, 1961, p. 125 no. 14 and Pl. 4; *TAM*, V, 1, 538.

Inscription: Διὶ Σαβαζίῳ
                 Ἀριοῦς Θεοφ(ί)-
                 λου Σαρδιανὸς
                 τόν τε οἶκον καὶ
               5 τὸν περικείμε-
                 νον τῷ οἴκῳ ψι-
                 λὸν τόπον ἀνέ-
                 θηκεν.

Coloe?: Kula

40.   A stele of grey marble, with a relief representing a pair of eyes and a pair of pigeons. It was copied by W. H. Buckler in June 1914, at which time it was in private hands.

Dimensions: height 0.66; width at top 0.32, at bottom 0.42; thickness 0.06.

W. H. Buckler, *ABSA* 21, 1914-16, p. 169 f.; Hermann, *Ergebnisse*, p. 51; *TAM*, V, 1, 264.

Inscription: Διεὶ Σαβαζίῳ καὶ Μη-
                 τρὶ Εἴπτα Διοκλῆς
                 Τροφίμου, ἐπεὶ ἔπει-
                 ασα περιστερὰς τῶν
               5 θεῶν ἐκολάσθην ἰς
                 τοὺς ὀφθαλμοὺς καὶ
                 ἐνέγραψα τὴν ἀρετήν.

41.   A stele commemorating the introduction of Sabazius cult. Only the top part, with the relief, is now preserved. The relief, in two registers, shows top center a man making a libation on a raised altar; to the right three worshippers looking left with their right hands raised and to the left a chariot drawn by two galloping horses, while a person seated in the chariot holds the reins. Above the horses there is an eagle and below them a snake, while behind them there is a figure holding a caduceus, and a crescent near this figure's head. In the lower register, a tree and an altar with offerings are to be seen in the middle, while to the left there are several worshippers facing right, and to the right six worshippers facing left. The stele was first seen by A. Wagener about 1855, and the preserved portion of it is now in the Manisa Museum, inv. no. 105.

Dimensions: present height 0170; width 0.63; thickness 0.08.

> A. Wagener, *Mémoires Couronnées par l'Académie de Belgique* 30, 1861, p. 3 no. 1; Keil and von Premerstein, *Zweite Reise*, p. 84, with listing of preceding bibliography; Cook, *Zeus*, 2 i, p. 284; L. Robert, *Hellenica* 6, 1948, p. 111-3; *TAM*, V, 1, 193.

Inscription: Ἔτους ρπε´ μη(νὸς) Δαισίου α´ ἐπὶ στεφανη-
φόρου Γλύκωνος ἡ Κολοηνῶν κατοικία κα-
θιέρωσεν Δία Σαβάζιον, ἐπὶ ἱερέων Ἀπολλωνίου τοῦ Ἰόλλα καὶ Ἀπολλωνίου τοῦ Δαίπ-
5   του Αἰσώπου καὶ Μητρᾶ Ἀσκληπιάδου καὶ
[Ἀρτε]μιδώρου Κλέωνος καὶ Κλέωνος Με-
[..... καὶ Ἀ]πολλωνίου Δίωνος καὶ Ἀ-

101 A.D.

Philadelphia Lydiae: Alaşehir

42.   A plaque of marble with a relief representing a standing man who is pouring a liquid from a patera into a crater. Behind the crater there is a tree. Known to Rayet, but not by sight, before 1877, and seen by Keil and von Premerstein at time of second journey.

Dimensions: height 0.595; width at top 0.37, at bottom 0.39; thickness 0.06.

> *Mouseion kai Bibliotheke*, I, B, p. 120, no. κα´; *BCH* 1, 1877, p. 307-9; Buresch, *Aus Lydien*, p. 75; Keil and von Premerstein, *Zweite Reise*, p. 84 no. 2; Cook, *Zeus*, 2 i, p. 285.

Inscription: Διὶ Κορυφαίῳ Δία Σα-
ουάζιον Νεαυλίτην
Πλουτίων Πλουτίωνος
Μαίων εὐχήν.

Ormeleis: Karamanlı

43.   A quadrangular basis, broken into three pieces, originally surmounted by a round column. The largest fragment was first seen by Collignon before 1877, and the entire stone by J. R. S. Sterrett in 1884, again by Ramsay in 1886.

> BCH 2, 1878, p. 243; Sterrett, *Epigraphical Journey*, p. 53-57 nos. 44-46; Ramsay, *Cities and Bishoprics*, p. 310 no. 127.

Inscription: 'Αγαθῇ Τύχῃ. "Ετους ρπβ,
                    οἱ μύσται τοῦ Διὸς Σαουαζ[ίου]
                    ὑπὲρ σωτηρίας αὐτῶν καὶ
                    τοῦ δήμου 'Ορμηλέων καὶ σω[τ-]
        5 ηρίας 'Αννίας Φαυστείνης
                    καὶ Τιβερίου Κλαυδίου ἐ-
                    πιτρόπου Κριτοβούλου, ἐπὶ
                    πραγματευτῶν 'Αβασκάν-
                    του καὶ 'Ανθίνου καὶ Μαρκ-
      10 ελλίωνος, ἐπὶ μισθωτῶν
                    [Κλαυδ]ίου 'Αβασκάντου καὶ
                    [Μήνιδ]ος Νεικάδου Ἡρα-
                    [κλεί]δου καὶ Νεικάδου δίς,
                    [ἱερα]τεύοντος Κιδραμά-
      15 [ντος] δὶς καὶ 'Ελπίδος τῆς
                    [γυ]ναικὸς αὐτοῦ, Μῆνις Δι-
                    [ομ]ήδου, 'Οσαὶς 'Αττάλου ἱε-
                    [ρε]ὺς Ἑρμοῦ, Μάρκιος δὶς Μη-
                    [ν]ογένου, "Ενθεος Κρατερο-
      20 [ῦ Σ]υμάχου ἱερεὺς Διονύσου,
                    [Μ]ῆνις 'Αττάλου Μουνδίω-
                    [ν]ος, "Ατταλος Δημητρίου,
                    [Μ]ῆνις 'Ατειμήτου, 'Ισπάτα-
                    [λ]ος Μήνιδος, "Ενθεος Μήνιδ-
      25 [ο]ς, Μῆνις Ποσιδωνίου "Ενθ-
                    [εο]ς, "Αχεπτος Μήνιδος, 'Οσαὶ[ς]
                    [Γ]λαύχου, Μῆνις Νεικολάου
                    Κιβυράτου, Μενιστεὺς Μήνι-
                    δος Μενιστέως, Νέαρχος Μήνιδ-
      30 ο[ς], Νέαρχος Νειχολάου Κιβυράτ[ου],
                    Αὐρήλλιος
                    Κιδραμᾶς τρὶς ἱερεὺς Δ-
                    ιὸς Σαυαζίου καὶ ἡ γυ-
                    νὴ αὐτοῦ "Αρτεμεις,

35 [Α]ὑρήλλιος Αὐρήλλιος
["Ατ]ταλος 'Οσαεὶ ἱερε-
[ὺς Ἑρ]μοῦ, 'Οσαεὶς 'Ατ-
[τάλου.]

207-8 A.D., if in Cibyratic Era

Aglanköy, in the vicinity of Cibyra

44. A red column with capital, first seen by W. M. Ramsay in 1884. The dimensions are unknown.

J. R. S. Sterrett, *Epigraphical Journey*, p. 37-38 no. 37; Ramsay, *Cities and Bishoprics*, p. 272 no. 97; *AJA* 3, 1887, p. 263; *BCH* 24, 1900, p. 61 bottom.

Inscription: Μῆνις 'Απολων[ί-]
                 ου ἑαυτῷ ζῶν
                 καὶ Νάνα τῇ γυναικὶ
                 ζώσῃ
             5   ἱερεὺς Δήμητρος
                 καὶ Σαοάζου.

Note: Ramsay also restores the name of Sabazius into Sterrett, *EJ* no. 81 = *Cities and Bishoprics*, p. 305 no. 101 on the analogy of this one.

Fig. 1

Tlos: Düver

44a. Two fragments of a limestone altar built into the east wall of the citadel. It was first recorded by Charles Fellows in 1840.

Dimensions: height (upper part) 0.38, (lower part) 0.28; width 0.72; lettes 0.02.

C. Fellows, *An Account of Discoveries in Lycia*, London 1841, p. 388 no. 128; *CIG* 4239; *TAM* II, 582; J. and L. Robert, *Fouilles d'Amyzon en Carie* I, Paris 1983, p. 175.

Inscription: [Τλωέων τῆς μητροπόλεως του]
[Λυκίων ἔθνους ἡ βουλὴ καὶ ὁ]
δῆμος ἐτείμησεν] . . . .

. . . .

. . . . [καὶ σειτήσει
ἐν πρυτανείωι, ἄνδρα ἀγαθὸν γε-
γονότα καὶ διὰ προγόνων εὐεργέ-
την τοῦ δήμου καὶ πολλὰ τῶν
συμφερόντων καὶ τὰ μέγιστα
5 π]ρὸς δόξαν κατερ[γ]ασμένον (sic)
τ]ῶι δήμωι καὶ τῶι Λυκίων ἔθνει
κ]αὶ ἐν τοῖς πολέμοις ἐπάνδρως
ἀ]γωνισάμενον καὶ ἀριστεύσαν-
τα καὶ διατηρήσαντα τούς τε νό-
10 μους καὶ τὴν πάτριον δημοκρατί-
αν καὶ ἱερατεύοντ[α] διὰ βίου πρὸ πό-
λ]εως Σ[α]β[ά]ζου (sic) φιλοδόξως καὶ με-
γαλομερῶς καὶ ἐν πάσῃ τῆι πολει-
τείᾳ καὶ κακοπαθῶς καὶ ἐπιτυχῶς
15 καὶ δικαίως ἀναστρεφόμενον.

Ca. 100 B.C.
The Roberts' discussion concerns the phrase πρὸ πόλεως, which indicates that we are dealing with an official god who protects the city. Cf. the same phrase in no. 27, above.

Unknown provenience, probably Asia Minor

45. Stele of bluish marble, with representation of Zeus-Sabazius on horseback with chiton, chlamys, and diadem, holding thunderbolt and two spears, approaching a leafless tree from the left. Around the tree is a snake, and on one branch is an eagle. At the base of the tree are an altar and a crater. It was purchased by W. H. Buckler in Constantinople in June, 1914, and is now in the British Museum.

Dimensions: height 0.34; width at top 0.36, at bottom 0.365; depth of panel 0.015; thickness 0.04 to 0.06.

A. B. Cook, *Zeus*, 2 i, pp. 282-5 and Pl. XIX; L. Robert, *Hellenica* 7, 1949, p. 56 note 6; *Bulletin of Museum of Fine Arts, Boston* 56, 1958, p. 72; Tacheva-Hitova, *Eastern*

Cults, no. III 22; C. Picard, *RA* 1961 (2), p. 166 and Fig. 14 falsely indicates that it is in the Istanbul Museum.

Inscription: Εὔτυχος Δὶ Σαβαζείῳ
κατ' ὄνιρον χαριστήριον.

INSULAE MARIS AEGAEI

Rhodus: Rhodes, Greece

46. A stele of white marble, broken above and below, discovered during the excavations of 1963 in the S.W. necropolis at the settlement known as Kizil Tepe, on the property of Eleutherios Peros. The stone seems to have been an accessory to the graves of the Sabaziastai, which were located in that necropolis. The stone is now in the epigraphical depot of Rhodes, inv. no. 1240.

Dimensions: height 0.36; width at top 0.336, at bottom 0.365; thickness at top 0.069, at bottom 0.073; letters 0.009.

The excavation is briefly mentioned *Archaiologikon Deltion* 19, 2, iii (1964), p. 473. A full treatment is now available in V. Kontorini, *Rhodiaka* I, Louvain 1983, 71-79.

Inscription: [...................]ν̣ παρέχεται οὐθέ̣-
να καιρὸν διαλείπων ἕνεκεν τῶν κοινῶν
πραγμάτων. ὅπως οὖν καὶ τὸ κοινὸν τὸ
Σαβαζιατᾶν φαίνηται καταξίας χάρι-
τας ἀποδίδον τοῖς εὐεργετεῖν αὐτὸ προ-
αιρουμένοις καὶ πολλοὶ τήν αὐτὴν αἵρε-
σιν ἔχωσιν v Ἀρίστωνι θεωροῦντες τὴν πα̣-
ρὰ τοῦ πλήθους εὐχαριστίαν, v κυρωθέν-
τος τοῦδε τοῦ ψηφίσματος, τύχηι ἀγαθῆι,
δεδόχθαι Σαβαζιαστᾶν τῶι κοινῶι ἐπαινέ-
σαι καὶ στεφανῶσαι εἰς τὸν ἀεὶ χρὸνον
Ἀρίστωνα Συρακόσιον θαλλίνωι στεφάνωι
ἀρετῆς ἕνεκεν καὶ ἐπιμελείας τῆς περὶ
τοὺς τάφους. v οἱ δὲ ἐπιμήνιοι ἢ ὁ ἐπιστάτας
οἱ ἀεὶ λειτουργοῦντες τὴν ἀνακήρυξιν τήν̣-
δε ποιείσθωσαν μετὰ τὴν ἐν τῶι ἀνδρῶνι
καθ' ἕκας̣τον ἐνιαυτὸν ο[.........νεκυ-]
σίοις ἐπάναγκες, μὴ πλέ̣[ον λογισάμενοι τῶι]
κοινῶι εἰς τὸν στέφα̣[νον δραχμᾶν ....]

The letter-forms point to a date at the end of the second or beginning of the first century B.C.

Thera: Thera (Santorini)

47. A votive tablet of marble, found by Hiller von Gaertringen before 1898 "ad viam, quae est supra Basilicam, in introitu casae privatae," now in archaeological museum of Thera.

Dimensions: height 0.17; length 0.31; thickness 0.09.

IG, XII iii, 142

Inscription: Σαβαζί[ῳ.....]

Dated by the editor to the second century B.C., but not entirely convincingly.

Delus: Delos

48. A stone re-employed as a threshold block, broken in two pieces. It was found in the excavations of 1909 in a house northwest of the Agora of Theophrastus. It is now on the terrace in front of the French excavation house, inv. no. 544. The piece seems originally to have been an architrave, and the letters on the right half are deliberately obliterated.

Dimensions: height 0.33; length 1.68; letters 0.028 to 0.030.

> Roussel and Hatzfeld, *BCH* 33, 1909, p. 511; *Inscriptions de Delos*, 2417; C. Vatin, *BCH* 91, 1967, pp. 447-50; *SEG* XXIV, 1160; *Bull. Ep.* 1963, no. 228; *Bull. Ep.* 1969, no. 410.

Inscription: Δειεὶ Σαβαζίῳ κ[αὶ.............]
                κατ᾽ εὐχὴν Μου[σωνίου 'Ρούφου...]
                τοῦ γεγονότος [ἱερέως διὰ βίου 'Απόλλωνος]
                ἐν Δήλῳ < Αἰλ.< ['Αλεξάνδρου]
    5   [ἄρχοντος]

To be dated to the reign of Antoninus Pius on prosopographical grounds.

Sicinus: Sikinos

49. A small basis, unworked on all sides, found before 1837 near the cemetery of the old city, in the house of I. Korteses. Now apparently lost. The dimensions are not recorded.

> Ross, *Archaiologia tes nesou Sikinou* (1837), p. 37 no. 4; *CIG* II Addenda, 2447a; *IG*, XII v, 27, with additional bibliography.

Inscription: 'Ετέαρχος 'Αρμύ[λου......]
                Σαβαζ[ίῳ]

AEGYPTUS

Oxyrrhynchus: El Behnesa

50. A fragment of papyrus in handwriting said to be that of the third cen-

tury A.D., found in the excavations of 1897-1906.
Dimensions: height 0.055; width 0.095

Poxy 33, 1968, 2678.

Inscription:　　ἐρωτᾷ σε Διοσχορούς δειπνῆ-
σαι εἰς γάμους τοῦ υἱοῦ τῇ ιδ´
τοῦ Μεσορὴ ἐν τῷ Σαβαζείῳ
ἀπὸ ὥρ(ας) θ´ διευτύχει.

GRAECIA

Peiraeus: Piraeus

51. A stele of Pentelic marble, broken in two pieces and incomplete at
bottom. At the top, there is a pediment with acroteria. It is said to have been
found by chance in January 1884, and is now in the Epigraphical Museum of
Athens, inv. no. 7844. The stele shows signs of having been re-engraved, and
in the opinion of Prof. Sterling Dow was originally used in the late 4th century
B.C.
Dimensions: height 1.39, width 0.37; thickness 0.03; letters 0.008.

Koumanoudes, *Arch. Eph.* 1883, p. 245 ff.; *IG* II v, 626b; *IG* II², 1325; Michel,
Recueil, no. 972; Ziebarth, *Vereinswesen*, p. 37.

Inscription:　　　　Θεο[ί]
'Αγαθεῖ τύχηι, ἐπὶ Θεοκλέους ἀρχον-
τος Μουνιχιῶνος ἀγορᾶι κυρίαι
ἔδοξεν τοῖς Σαβαζιασταῖς ἀνα-
5 γράψαι τὰ ὀνόματα τῶν ἐρανι-
στῶν ἐν στήληι λιθίνηι καὶ στῆσαι
ἐν τῷ ἱερῷ.
ἱερεὺς
Ζήνων 'Αντιοχεὺς
10 ταμίας καὶ
γραμματεὺς
καὶ ἐπιμελητὴς
Δωρόθεος "Οαθεν
ἐρανισταὶ
15 Εὔβουλος Σημαχίδης
Βάκχιος Μιλήσιος
Ξενοκλείδης Σουνιεὺς
Διοκλῆς Κολωνῆθεν
"Επαινος Φαληρεὺς νε(ώτερος)
20 Σωμένης Οἰναῖος

Ἔπαινος Φαληρεὺς πρεσ(βύτερος)
Διογένης Μακεδών
Φαῖδρος Μιλήσιος
Διογένης Ἀμφιτροπῆθεν
25 Ἀπελλῆς Κολωνῆθεν
Ἀπολλόδωρος Ξυπεταιών
Θεοδόσιος Ἀχαρνεύς
Κόιντος Προβαλίσιος
30 Ἀρτέμων Λαοδικεύς
Διονύσιος Λαοδικεύς
Δημήτριος Ἀντιοχεύς
Διόδοτος Ἁλιμούσιος
Διονύσιος Ἁλιμούσιος
35 Ἀθηνόδοτος Οἰναῖος
Μενέδημος Μακεδών
Σήραμβος Αἰθαλίδης
Θεοδόσιος Ἁγνούσιος
Ζώβιος Ἡρακλεώτης
40 Διονύσιος Φλιεύς
Εὐφρώνιος Φαληρεύς
Εὐρύστρατος Κικχυνεύς
Ἀθηνόδοτος Οἰναῖος πρε(σβύτερος)
Διονύσιος Ἕρμειος
45 Σῶσος Μαρωνίτης
Φίλων
Λῦσις Παλληνεύς
Πλούταρχος Αἰγινίτης
Ἀριστοτέλης Παιανεύς
50 Ὠκυμένης Προβαλίσιος
Πόθων
Πολέμαρχος Φαληρεύς
Σωσιγένης Προβαλίσιος
Ῥόδιππος Ῥαμνούσιος
55 Σωσιγένης Ἀπαμεύς
Φιλόστρατος Κολωνῆθεν
Μενέμαχος Παιανεύς
Ἀγαθοκλῆς δημόσιος
60 Δημήτριος Ἀλωπεκῆθεν
Ληναῖος Μιλήσιος
Θέων Ὄῃθεν
Σωτᾶς Ἀναγυράσιος
Εὐβουλίδης
65 Δημήτριος Ἁμαξαντεύς

[ἀνεγρά]φη ἐπὶ Μηδείου Μουνιῶνος.

101-100 B.C., according to the chronology given in Dinsmoor, *The Athenian Archon List in the Light of Recent Discoveries*, but recording the membership of two years previously.

52. Perhaps to be associated with the preceding, if we can assume cult-continuity without documentation for a period of over two hundred years, is a statue base reputedly found at the same time and place. It is now in the Epigraphical Museum of Athens, inv. no. 8991.
Dimensions: height 0.09; length 0.34; thickness 0.50; letters 0.012.

Koumanoudes, *loc. cit.*; Michel, *Recueil*, no. 1038; *IG* II², 2932.

Inscription: οἵδε ἱεροποιήσαντες
ἔθεσαν ἐπὶ Σωσιγένος ἄρχον(τος)
Νίκων Εὐτυχίδης
Δημοκλῆς Μαντίθεος

342/1 B.C.

Epidaurus: Epidauros

53. A tablet of limestone, inscribed on both sides, found in the sanctuary of Asclepius before 1895. Now apparently lost.
Dimensions: height 0.50; width 0.37; thickness 0.24.

Blinkenberg, *Nordisk Tidskrift för Filologie* 3 iii, p. 166 no. 15; *IG* IV, 1057; *Arch. Eph.* 1913, p. 125 no. 4, adding second side; *IG* IV i², 395.

Inscription: Διὶ Σαβαζίῳ
Μηνόφιλος Ͻ
πυροφορήσας
τὸ ξγ´ ἔτος

5 [Διο]νύσιος Διο-
ν[υ]σίου πυροφο-
ρήσας.

186 A.D.

54. An altar of grey limestone, broken on the upper left and below, discovered at unspecified time in the excavations of the Asklepieion. Now in the annex of the Epidaurus Museum. It is inscribed on two sides. The typical Epidaurian circular symbol is imposed on the front of the stone.
Dimensions: height 0.37; width 0.19, thickness 0.20; letters ca. 0.026, but 0.012 in line 3.

W. Peek, *Neue Inschriften aus Epidauros*, Abhandlungen der sächsischen Akademie der Wissenschaften zu Leipzig, Phil.-Hist. Klasse 63 v, 1972, no. 61 and Pl. XVI, 37, without the last three lines, which are on the side of the stone.

Inscription: [Δ]ιὸς
              [Σα]βαζίου
              ['Α]πολλοφά-
              νης πυρο-
          5 φορ[ήσ]ας
              ἱερῖ 'Ονησι-
              φόρῳ Ɔ
              ἔτους
              traces

          10 [.]ΕΡΜΟ[...]
              [.] ΦΡΟΜΙ[..]
              OΥΡΑΝΙ[..]

1. 7: "Le sigle pour 'Ονησιφόρου" (J. and L. Robert, *Bull. Ep.* 1973, no. 190); see also in no. 53.

Argos: Argos

55. A long piece of marble, discovered ca. 1840, but now apparently lost. The dimensions are not recorded.

Ross, *Archäologische Zeitung* 2, 1844, p. 349; Le Bas and Foucart, *Voyage Archéologique*, II, 137; *IG* IV, 649.

Inscription: Α[ὐρ.] 'Απολλωνίδης
              [ἱερεὺς] Διὸς Σεβαζείου τὸ μνῆμα
              [κατεσχ]εύασεν ζῶν. Πο. 'Απολλωνί(δα) (Δί)ων χαίρετε
              [......]ιον ζήσασ(α) ἡλικία[ς] ἔτεσι τριάντα δύω Πολέταρ[χε]
         5 [......]α ῥαψωδὲ χαῖρε ζήσας ἔτη λ.

DALMATIA

Aenona: Nin

56. A votive altar of white limestone, its surface badly damaged by the sea. It was found October 2, 1950 in a field belonging to Ivo Ljubičić on the coast at Zdrijac near Nin, and is apparently still in the discoverer's house.

Dimensions: height 0.345; height of base 0.095, of moulding at top 0.045; width, top and bottom 0.24, inscribed surface 0.195; thickness 0.21; letters 0.023 in line 4 to 0.035 in line 5.

Mate Suić, *Vjesnik za arheologiju i historiju dalmatinsku* 53, 1950-51, p. 233-4; Julijan Medini, "Sabazijev Kult u Rimskoj Proviniji Dalmaciji/Sabazius' Cult in the Roman Province of Dalmatia", in *Vjesnik za arheologiju i historiju dalmatinsku* 74, 1980, p. 67-88 and Pl. XXVI, 2.

Inscription: Iovi Sab-
asio Iico
L. Plotius
Eperastus
5 V.S.L.M.

ITALIA

Roma: Rome

57. A marble altar found in 1885 during construction work on the site of the camp of the "equites singulares." It is now in the Museo Nazionale delle Terme, inv. no. 78187. It is inscribed on three sides.
Dimensions: height 0.68; maximum width 0.51.

Muenzer, *Annali* 1885, p. 273 no. 26; *Bull. Comun.* 1885, p. 155 no. 1082; *Notizie degli Scavi* 1885, p. 524; *CRAI* 1886, p. 33; *CIL* VI, 31164; Dessau, *ILS*, 2189.

Inscription (starting with left side and going around to the right):
Fl. Bassus Dec.
Fl. Valens Dupl.
Aelius Bonus Dupl.
Aurel. Vitalis Ducl. (*sic*)
5 Iulius Longinus Tab.
Aelius Severus Sig.
Aurelius Victor Tur.
Iulius Valentinus
Aurel. Pistus
10 Aurel. Sudius
Aurel. Mestrius
Aurel. Mucianus
Aurel. Diogenes
15 I. O. M.
Deo Sabadio sacrum
Iulius Faustus Dec. N.
Eqq. Sing. D.N. ex votum (*sic*)
posuit et conalarium
20 nomina inseruit
ex ala prima Darda. Prov. Moesiae Inf.

dedicata
IIII non. Aug.
Domino N. Gordiano Aug.
25 II et Pompeiano Coss.

1. 19: *conalaris* i.e. a member of the same *ala*.

2 Aug., 241 A.D.

58. A marble statuette of a seated goddess (Fortune or Abundance?) head, right forearm, and top of cornucopia missing. It was found in the course of construction work on the Victor Emmanuel monument in 1892. Now in Musei Capitolini, inv. no. 6723. The inscription is arranged in two columns.
Dimensions: height 0.36.

> Gatti, *Notizie degli Scavi* 1892, p. 344; *Bull. Comun.* 1892, p. 364; *CIL* VI, 30948; Dessau, *ILS*, 4088.

Inscription: Per voce(m)
                    Pegasi
                    sacerdot(is)
                    sancto deo Sabazi(o)
                5   d(ono)
                    Attia Celerina de[d(it).]

59. A marble tablet, found under the Capitoline in 1889. Now in the Musei Capitolini, inv. no. 6738.
Dimensions: height 0.49; width 0.27; thickness 0.06.

> *Notizie degli Scavi* 1889, p. 225; Gatti, *Bull. Comun.* 1889, p. 437; *CIL* VI, 30949; Dessau, *ILS*, 4089.

Inscription: M. Furius
                    Clarus
                    pro salute
                    filiorum suorum
                5   M. Aurel. Clari
                    et Furiae Clarae
                    [sa]ncto invicto
                    [Sa]bazi(o)
                10 [aram et M]ercurium
                    [donum dedi]t.

60. A plaque of marble found in 1939 by Prof. A. M. Colini in the area of the Forum Holitorium. Now in Musei Capitolini, inv. no. 2793.

Dimensions: height 0.345; width 0.18; thickness 0.03.

M. Guarducci, *Bull. Comun.* 1946-8, p. ,16 f.; Pietrangeli, *Musei Capitolini, I Monumenti dei Culti Orientali*, Roma 1951, p. 26 no. 5.

Inscription: [.Ca]ecilius Pra
                 [...]us con filio
                 [suo] A. Caecilio P
                 [....]co pro suam
           5   [salu]tem d. d. aque
                 [ins]trumentum
                 [deo sanc]to Sabazi(o) et
                 [Celesti]Triumphali.

The restoration of *Celesti* in the last line is based on another inscription, found in the same place, which uses *triumfalis* as an epithet of Caelestis (= Tanit).

61.   An altar decorated with garlands and ram's heads. It was discovered in Renaissance times in the transtiburtine area of Rome, transported to Florence, and subsequently lost.

CIL VI, 429 (with earlier bibliography); Dessau, *ILS*, 4086.

Inscription: Iovi Sabaz(io)
                 Q. Nunnius
                 Alexander
                 v.s.l.m.

This altar is now in the Detroit Institute of Arts, and has been there since 1937 (acc. no. 37.185). Stylistically, it is to be assigned a Flavian date. Dimensions: height 0.69; width 0.44; thickness 0.28.

P. Visonà, *ZPE* 52, 1983, p. 79-82.

62.   A small base of white marble, discovered in Renaissance times in the transtiburtine area of Rome, and subsequently lost. The dimensions are unknown.

CIL VI, 430, (with earlier bibliography); Dessau, *ILS*, 4087; *Inscriptiones Italiae* X 4, 387 (followed by V. Kolsev, *Arheoloski Vestnik* 19, 1968, p. 280) confusedly cites this piece as being from Trieste, now lost.

Inscription: Q. Nunnius
                 Alexander
                 donum dedit
                 Iovi Sabazio.

63.   A stone tablet known at least since 1795, but now apparently lost. The dimensions are not recorded.

> *CIL* VI, 30950, with earlier bibliography: Dessau, *ILS*, 4090.

Inscription: magna dunam[is....]
Sabazzi, Servilia[......]
parum videor mag[nitudinem]
tuam dic[tis aequare posse]

64.   A small altar with low relief work on all four sides. Known since 1873, but now apparently lost. It has the following representations: in the front, Artemis sitting left on a rock, her foot on a deer's neck. Her right hand touches a tree's branches, and in her left she holds an upside-down torch. She wears a hunting costume. On the right side, there is a nude Apollo, his legs crossed, his left arm resting on a lyre which in turn is on an altar. His right hand is held up over his head, and there are trees on either side. On the left side there is a Dionysus-like character (*not* Sabazius, as has generally been thought) in a long gown, walking on his toes, holding in the left hand a thyrsus-like spear decorated with ribbons, and placing the right hand on his head. To the left there is a pine and to the right a cypress. On the back there is a water-bird on a rock under a pine-tree, with a long object in front of its beak. The inscription is on a ledge under the front representation, and has laurel around the top.
Dimensions: height 0.15; relief-field 0.08; width 0.06; thickness 0.065.

> F. Matz and F. von Duhn, *Antike Bildwerke in Rom* III, Leipzig 1882, p. 143 no. 3763; *IG* XIV, 1021; *IGR* I, 98; Moretti, *Inscriptiones Graecae Urbis Romae* I, Roma 1968, no. 185.

Inscription: Πάρος Σαβαζί-
ῳ δῶρον.

65.   Inscriptions accompanying a variety of wall paintings in a catacomb. The monument has been known since the 18th century, but was first adequately published in 1852. It forms part of the largely Christian cemetery of Praetextatus off the Via Appia, and now appears to be sealed off and inaccessible. The dimensions are irrelevant.

> Among the extensive bibliography I single out, Rossi, *Bulletino* 1853, p. 87 ff.; *CIL* VI, 142 (which also contains a Mithraic inscription in an adjoining room); Cumont, *CRAI* 1906, p. 72 f.; W.O.E. Oesterley, "The Cult of Sabazius, a Study in Syncretism," in *The Labyrinth*, ed. S. H. Hooke; Nilsson, *GGR* II², p. 663. For the complete bibliography, see M. J. Vermaseren; *De onderlinge betrekkingen tussen Mithras-Sabazius-Cybele* in *Academiae Analecta*, Brussels 1984, p. 34 ff.

Inscription: accompanying wall painting for which the reader is referred to the plates:

Dis Pater   Aera Cura
       Fata Divina
Mercurius Nuntius
Vibia Alcestis
5 abreptio Vibies et descensio
septe(m) pii Sacerdotes
       Vincentius
bonorum iudicio iudicati
       Vibia
10   angelus
       bonus
inductio Vibies
[Vi]ncenti hoc o[pus re]quetes quot vides. Plures me antecesserunt, omnes expecto
Manduca, vibe, lude, et beni ad me. Cum vibes, bene fac. Hoc tecum feres.
15 Numinis antistes Sabazis Vincentius hic e[st q]ui sacra sancta
       deum mente pia coluit.

Ostia: Ostia

66.   A marble tablet, broken into several pieces. It was found in 1909 in a shrine, variously identified as a Sabazius-sanctuary or a Mithraeum. It is now in the Ostia lapidarium, inv. no. 8194.

Dimensions: height 0.161, width 0.355; thickness 0.045; letters 0.022 to 0.029.

Vaglieri, *Notizie degli Scavi* 1909, p. 22 no. 1; *CRAI* 1909, p. 189; *Ephemeris Epigraphica* 9, 439; *CIL* XIV, 4296; Vermaseren, *CIMRM* I, 303; Squarciapino, *I Culti orientali ad Ostia*, EPRO 3, Leiden 1962, p. 65 f.

Inscription: L. Aemiliu[s......]
       Eusc(hemus?) ex imperio Iov-
       is Sabazi votum fecit.

Suessula: Castellone

67.   A base of travertine, found on the hill called Carvignano (between Maddaloni and Cervina) in 1733. Now in Naples Museum, inv. no. 3622. On the sides are reliefs representing an urceus and a patera.

Dimensions: height 1.50; width 0.84.

CIL X, 3764; Dessau, *ILS*, 6341; V. Tran Tam Tinh, *Le Culte des divinités orientales en Campanie*, EPRO 27, Leiden 1972, p. 121 no. C28, with other bibliography.

Inscription (interpretation of Tran Tam Tinh):
       L(ucio) Pompeio Felicissimo

immuni dendr(ophoro) Suessul(ae)
et sacerdoti M(atris) D(eum) XVvir(ali) in
vico Novanensi, patri L(ucii)
5 Pompei Felicissimi decur(ioni) et
IIvir(o) et q(uaestori) alim(entario) et omnibus
rebus ac munerib(us) perfu-
ncto, cultores I(ovis) O(ptimi) M(aximi) S(abazii)
Hortensens patron(o)
10 b(ene) m(erito) ob sing(ularem) erga se libe-
ralitatem et prae-
stantiam l(oc̦o) d(ato) d(ecreto) (decurionum).

Comparison with nos. 55 and 75 seems to justify the interpretation of the inscription as referring to Sabazius.

Casinum: Cassino

68. A stone of unknown description first seen in the 17th century but lost already by 1734. The dimensions are unrecorded.

CIL X, 5197; Dessau, ILS, 4093.

Inscription: L. Luccio L. f. Ter.
Hibero
IIvir(o) iter(um) QQ patrono
Sacerdoti Sacror(um) Savadior(um)
5   cur(atori) r(ei) p(ublicae) Interamnat. Liren.
eorund(em) et patrono
iudici CCCC selecto
Casinates publ(ica) ob merita eius
d(ederunt) d(edicaverunt)

Capranica Prenestina, near ancient Praeneste

69. A marble tablet, known at least since 1865. The exact findspot is unclear. I have been unable to determine its present whereabouts. The dimensions are unrecorded. An oak wreath surrounds the middle two lines of the inscription.

Henzen, Bulletino 1866, p. 137; CIL XIV, 2894; Dessau, ILS, 4092.

Inscription: Deo magno Silvano Marti Herculi
Iovi
Zabazio
Antullus

Fiano Romano, near ancient **Capena**

70.   A rectangular block of marble, said in 1905 to be in the courtyard of the former ducal palace. I have been unable to determine its present whereabouts.

Dimensions: height 0.38; width 0.25; thickness 0.25.

> *Notizie degli Scavi* 1905, p. 363; Dessau, *ILS*, 9277.

Inscription: Iovi Sabazo
                  optimo et
                  Fortunae
                  sanctae
           5   M. Caerellius
                  Sossius
                  ex viso
                  [don]um dedit.

Viterbo, in the vicinity of ancient **Sorrina**

71.   A stone of unknown description, bearing between the two portions of the inscription, a relief showing a horseman to the right, a boar, a dog, and a tree. It was seen by Bormann in 1910 and 1912 in the house of the Gentile family, but may be originally from Rome. I have been unable to determine its present whereabouts. The dimensions are unrecorded.

> *CIL* VI, 37187.

Inscription: D(eo) Sa(ncto) Iovi Sabazio

                 Val(erius) Aulusanus mil(es) c(o)hor(tis)
                 II pre 7 Merca[t]oris V.S.L.[M.]

Luna: Luni

72.   A stone of unknown description, known since 1442, when it was seen by Cyriacus of Ancona. In 1610 reported as built into wall under campanile of church of the hospital of San Lazzaro. Now apparently lost. The dimensions are unrecorded.

> *CIL* XI, 1323, with earlier bibliography and variant readings.

Inscription: St. Metti-
                  us Zethus
                  Iovi
                  Sabazio
           5   d(onum) l(ibens) d(edit)
                  l(oco) d(ato) d(ecreto) d(ecurionum).

AFRICA

Belalis Major: Henchir el-Fouar

73.   An altar with inscription in recessed field. On either side of the field there is a thyrsus, and over it a wreath. It was found by Amar Mahjoubi in the course of excavations in 1960, built into a late wall. I do not know where it is now housed.

Dimensions: height 0.98; width 0.56.

Mahjoubi, *CRAI*, 1960, pp. 387-90.

Inscription: Ex iusso Iov(is)
                Zabazi
                ara posit(a)
                Libero Patr(i)
                cura
            5   M. Oppi Vitali.

GALLIA

Aquae Calidae: Vichy

74.   A plaque of silver foil, shaped more or less to resemble a tree. At the bottom, there is an aedicula with a representation of Jupiter standing, holding scepter and thunderbolt, an eagle at his feet. Below the representation is a tabula ansata with the inscription. In spite of repeated publications, the dimensions do not seem to have been recorded. It was found together with 79 similar but uninscribed plaques in the winter of 1864-5. Now it is in the Museum of St. Germain-en-Laye.

C. Rossignol and A. Bertrand, *Bulletin de la Societé d'Émulation du départment de l'Allier, Sciences, Arts, Belles Lettres* 18, 1889, pp. 185-232 and Pls. 1-8; *CIL* XIII, 1496; Cook, *Zeus* 2 i, p. 285-6 fig. 185; Dessau, *ILS*, 4091; A. Morlet, *Vichy Gallo-romain*, Mâcon 1957, pp. 280-4; C. Picard, *Revue Archéologique du Centre* 1, 1962, p. 10ff.

Inscription: Numin. Aug. Deo Iovi Sa-
                basio G. Iul. Caras-
                sounus V.S.L.M.

Found in the same archaeological context as a coin of Gordian III.

Such foil plaques are encountered also in the cult of Jupiter Dolichenus (*cf.* A. Kan, *Juppiter Dolichenus*, Leiden 1943, Pl. 8), a god to whom Sabazius is iconographically similar. Indeed, if one has a figurine of a bearded divinity with Phrygian cap, it is impossible to know to which of the two it should be attributed, in the absence of other characteristics. *Cf.*, e.g. Popović, *Antička bronza u Jugosloviji*, Belgrade 1969, 99 no. 125.

GERMANIA SUPERIOR

Mogontiacum: Mainz

75. An altar of yellow sandstone, first found in the district of Mombach in 1525, and relocated in the course of razing part of the Mainz city-wall at Eisgrubenweg in 1886. Taken to the Mittelrheinisches Landesmuseum, but not to be found there now.
Dimensions: height 0.75; width 0.55; thickness 0.33.

> Brambach, *CIRh*, 972, with further bibliography: Keller, *Westdeutsche Zeitschrift* 6, 1887, p. 80; *CIL* XIII, 6708; Dessau, *ILS*, 2294, E. Schwertheim, *Die Denkmäler orientalischer Gottheiten im römischen Deutschland*, EPRO 40, Leiden 1974, pp. 122-3, no. 104.

Inscription: I.O.M.
               Sabasio
               Conservatori
               honori Aquilae
      5 leg. XXII pr(imigeniae) p(iae) f(idelis)
               [Alexandr]i̯ana̯e̯
               M. Aur. Germanus
               d(omo) Emone
               ....

Reign of Alexander Severus, 222-235 A.D. (the only period during which the legion bore the name *Alexandriana*, erased after the emperor's *damnatio*).

UNCERTAIN PROVENIENCE

76. A bronze boar on a base-plate, acquired by the British Museum from the Weber sale in 1919.
Dimensions: height 0.055; length 0.075.

> Cook, *Zeus* 3, p. 874 note 15; *Bull. Ep.* 1941, no. 17a.

Inscription: Μυρτίνη θεῷ Σαβαζίῳ.

NON-INSCRIBED MONUMENTS, EXCLUDING HANDS AND STATUETTES ONCE ASSOCIATED WITH HANDS

PROVINCIAE ASIAE MINORIS

Augustapolis: Çavdarli, east of Afyon Karahissar

77. A statue of the god, placing his right foot on a ram's head. Next, to the left, there is a large frog. The statue was found in the course of non-archaeological excavations in 1964. Its context is that of a sanctuary, in which statues of Cybele and of various classical gods were also found. The piece is now in the Museum of Afyon Karahissar, No. E 1908, 441a, awaiting formal publication.

Dimensions: height ca. 0.60.

> Rudolf Fellmann, "Der Sabazios-Kult," in *Die orientalischen Religionen im Römerreich*, EPRO 93, Leiden 1981, p. 321. Additional information furnished by letter from Dr. Fellmann.

This piece is now accessible in the exhibition catalogue, *The Anatolian Civilizations, II, Greek, Roman, Byzantine*, Istanbul 1983, no. B 346. The height is stated to be 0.93.

MOESIA INFERIOR

Fîntînele, near Constanța (ancient **Tomis**), Romania

78. A rectangular plaque of marble with raised border. It shows, in the center, Sabazius standing frontally, his right hand outstretched, holding an indistinct object. His left hand is upraised to hold a staff topped by a ram's head. To the viewer's right of the standing figure are, left to right, a ladder with five rungs (thought by the editor perhaps to have something to do with five stages of initiation), a tree, and a snake. Immediately to the viewer's left of the standing figure is a crook (pedum), and farther to the left, from bottom to top, are an altar with fire on it; two indistinct oblong, slightly bent objects; and a man plowing with a yoke of lions, while a raven looks on. At various places in the field there are various other, mostly circular, indistinct objects.

The plaque was discovered accidentally, in the course of agricultural work, during the winter of 1977-8, in the center of the ancient settlement to the N.W. of the village of Fîntînele. The resemblance of this piece to the Copenhagen, Berlin, and Ampurias plaques, to be discussed below (nos. 80-82, 85) puts the identification as Sabazius out of question.

Dimensions: height 0.242; width 0.235; thickness 0.027.

> Al. Suceveanu, *Studii şi Cercetâri de Istorie Veche şi Arheologie* 31, 1980, 572-579.

GRAECIA

Argos: Argos

79. A stele of greyish marble, with a bearded rider wearing chlamys, chiton, and Phrygian cap. He holds an indistinct object in his right hand, which is held out over the horse's head. In front of him there is a tree around which a snake is twined. A branch protrudes from the top of the tree and terminates in what appears to be a bunch of leaves. Between the horse and tree stands an attendant, holding a torch partially obscured by the horse's right forefoot. Although the general motif of rider (usually, however, youthful), snake-entwined tree and attendant is widespread, e.g. in the Thracian-rider reliefs, the combination of the similarity of this piece to no. 45 above, the rider's beard and Phrygian cap (usual on the statuettes or busts on the votive hands), and the epigraphic attestation of Sabazius in Argos lead me to the conclusion that Sabazius is intended to be represented.

Dimensions: 0.43; width 0.295; thickness, 0.088.

> Unpublished. Circumstances of discovery unknown. Now in Argos Museum, without inventory no.

Macedonia or Epirus
Exact provenience unknown

79a. A bronze votive tablet, in the form of an aedicula, now in the archaeological museum of Tirana, Albania. Pending a forthcoming publication by Dr. Rudolf Fellmann, I restrict myself to a brief notice.

Dimensions: width 0.22; height of main field 0.255; diagonal border of gable 0.16.

> Sörries, *Antike Welt* 14, iv, 1983, pp. 20 (photo) and 24 (text).

ITALIA

ROMA: Rome

80. A bronze tablet, originally plated with tin, and apparently once soldered to a stronger piece of metal. It has been known since 1886. It appears to have been originally from Rome, and is now in the National Museum of Copenhagen. The decoration, in hammered relief, shows Sabazius standing in an aedicula. In the gable, there is Helios in a quadriga, and two stars. In the field, left and right over the aedicula, the Dioscuri. Sabazius is bearded, dressed in "Phrygian" costume, and has his right foot on a ram's head. In his outstretched right hand he holds a pine-cone, and in his left a scepter topped by a hand. At the bottom left, there is an altar which appears to be part of a building. At the bottom right there is a tree-trunk which also appears to be part of a building. A pine-branch seems to be growing out of the trunk. On the trunk there are a lizard, a snake, and an eagle with a wreath in its beak. To the upper left and right are Selene, Helios, and the caps of the Dioscuri. In addition, there are the following attributes, left, top to bottom: a scale, a fly, a haunch of meat, crossed flutes, thunderbolt, a mouse gnawing on the meat, a whip, a bull, a yoke, a crater, a club, a hydria, a rosette, a cornucopia; between Sabazius' legs: a turtle, a bee; to right, top to bottom: a grasshopper, two rosettes, an upside-down vessel, a caduceus, two cymbals, an ear of grain, a plow, and a frog.

Dimensions: height 0.232; width 0.156; thickness 0.0005.

Blinkenberg, p. 90 f and Pl. II; Nilsson, *GGR* II², Pl. 13 no. 2.

81. Two bronze plates, originally gilded. Hinged together, and with hinges for a third adjoining plate to the right. They were apparently intended as a chestpiece for a priest. They were acquired by the Berlin Antiquarium in 1891, and appear originally to be from Rome. The inv. nos. are 8169 and 8170. On the central plate we see Cybele seated on a throne, flanked by Hermes to the left and Attis to the right. Cybele has a turret-crown, a poppy, and a lion on her lap. Hermes has a petasus, a caduceus, and a bag behind his back. Attis has a flower. In the field there are cymbals and crossed flutes. Two diminutive figures on the back of the throne hold a wreath over Cybele's head. In the gable there is the quadriga of the sun. On the left plate, Sabazius stands to the left, his right leg somewhat raised. As on no. 64 he holds a pinecone and a scepter topped with a hand. An eagle and cymbals are in the pediment. The field contains a star, a bunch of grapes, a rosette, a caduceus, a whip, scales, flutes, a cornucopia, an altar with fire, offering cakes, a snake, a lizard, a fly, a bucranium, a turtle, and various indistinct objects.

Dimensions: diameter, 0.18.

Archäologischer Anzeiger 1892, p. 111; Blinkenberg, pp. 96-97; Vermaseren, *CCCA* III, no. 304.

82. A similar set of plates, known since 1826, likewise in the Berlin Antiquarium, inv. no. 8170 a and 8170 b. They are also apparently from Rome. The central plaque, at least, is so similar as certainly to be from the same mold, and this may be true of the side-plaque also. Unfortunately, they are in such poor condition as not to allow photography.

Bonner Jahrbücher 23, 1856, p. 52 and Pl. 3; Friederichs, *Berlins antike Bildwerke* II, no. 2005b; Blinkenberg, p. 96; Vermaseren *CCCA*, III, no. 304, with false indication that it is still in Bonn; G. Heres in *Forschungen und Berichte* 22, 1982, 195 and Pl. 29.

Volsinii: Bolsena

83. A bust of Sabazius in high relief. The god is bearded, and wears a Phrygian cap and a sleeved tunic. In his right hand he holds a pine-cone, and in his left a staff entwined by a snake. The piece is in the Vatican Museums, inv. no. 12159, from the collection of the Marchese Ravizza. There are nailholes in the corners.

Dimensions: height 0.27; width 0.23.

> Cumont, *RA*, 1892 I, p. 186 f. and Pl. 10; *Textes et Monuments*, II, no. 104b and fig. 98; Helbig, *Führer durch die öffentlichen Sammlungen klassischer Altertümer in Rom*, Tübingen 1963, no. 820; Blinkenberg, pp. 97-98; Nilsson, *GGR* II², Pl. 14 no. 2.

84. A somewhat similar bust-relief, with the same history as no. 83. It is now in the Vatican Museums, inv. no. 12158. Sabazius is represented bareheaded and barechested, except for a fold of cloak at his left shoulder. He holds a pine-cone and a branch, around which a snake is wound. There is an eagle on his right shoulder. Attributes, at the bottom of the piece, comprise an eight-part offering cake, a representation of Mithras killing the bull, a crater, and a ram's head. As in the case of no. 69, this piece has nailholes in the corners, but differs in being cast rather than hammered.

Dimensions: height 0.25; width 0.20.

> Cumont, *RA*, 1892 I, p. 186 f. and Pl. 10; Cumont, *Textes et Monuments*, II, no. 104 a and fig. 97; Helbig, *op. cit.*, no. 818; Blinkenberg, *loc. cit.*; Nilsson, *op. cit.*, Pl. 14 no. 1; Vermaseren, *CIMRM* I, no. 659 and fig. 185.

HISPANIA

Emporiae - Ampurias

85. Bronze plaques, once silvered, found in a child's grave in 1908 in the Necropolis of Ampurias, and now in the Gerona Museum. The larger plaque shows Sabazius bearded and facing, in Oriental costume, his right hand lifted in gesture of blessing, rays coming out of it. His left hand holds a scepter, but it cannot be determined whether it was originally topped with a votive hand. His right foot is placed on a ram's head, and there are three small two-handled craters between his feet. There is a tree to the viewer's left, with a snake around its trunk, foliage and grapes on the top, and a bust of Dionysus emerging from it. Superimposed on the tree are crossed thyrsi with a drum and small bells. On the other side is another tree, clearly a pine, with a crested snake wound around it, and farther to the right is a woodcutter with an axe. Under each tree is a semicircular niche. In the one to the left there is a woman making an offering on an altar. She is accompanied by a lizard and two turtles. In the one to the right, a woman holds a baby, and is accompanied by a bird and a reptile. At the upper left there are a moon and a star, but apparently the expectable balancing sun was never at the upper right. Going down the left side one sees a dagger, a winged caduceus and a flaming altar. In front of the altar is a large crater, and on it two Sabazius-hands are set up. Of the one preserved side plaque of a probably original two, there is a Dioscurus, nude but for cap and boots, with a horse, lance, and a star in the field. There are nailholes in both plaques.

Dimensions: height 0.318; width 0.275 (main plaque); height 0.30; width 0.14 (side plaque).

> C. Picard, *RA*, 1961 II, p. 156 and fig. 10; A. García y Bellido, *Les Religions orientales dans l'Espagne romaine*, EPRO 5, Leiden 1967, pp. 73-81.

GALLIA

Exact provenience unknown

86. A bronze figurine, of unknown circumstances of discovery. The divinity portrayed has a beard and mustache, and wears a Phrygian cap, a short tunica with sleeves, trousers, and a cape which hangs from his shoulders. In his outstretched right hand, he holds a pine-cone, and his left is raised, so as to have held a staff. Although this figurine is aberrant from the typical seated Sabazius-figurines which were intended for attachment to hands, there can be little doubt, considering its similarity to the Sabazius of the Copenhagen-plaque, but that our divinity is intended.

This piece is now in the Louvre, Paris, no. Bronze 699.

Dimensions: height 0.085.

> A. de Longperier, *Notice des bronzes antiques du Louvre*, Paris 1879, no. 422; S. Reinach, *Répertoire de la statuaire grecque et romaine*, Paris 1897-1910, 2, 478, 7; Blinkenberg, 98-99.

DALMATIA

Jadar (Diadora): Zadar, Jugoslavia

87. A mold for the production of hammered Sabazius-plaques, such as those of Copenhagen, Berlin, and Ampurias. The mold shows (in mirror-image negative) Sabazius standing turned to the viewer's left, within an aedicula, his right foot on a ram's head, his right hand holding a pine-cone, his left grasping a tree around which a snake is wound. The divinity is bearded, wears what may be a kalathos (modius) on his head, and is dressed in a short chiton. He appears to be barefoot. In the pediment of the aedicula is an eagle. The mold has been known since ca. 1965, and was found in the *favissae* of the Capitoline temple of Jader.

Dimensions: height 0.175; width 0.100; thickness 0.050.

M. Suić, "Orientalni kultovi u antičkom Zadru", in *Diadora* 3, 1965, 97-100, with
misidentification as Sarapis; Julijan Medini, "Sabazijev kult u rimskoj provinciji
Dalmaciji", in *Vjesnik za arheologiju i historiju dalmatinsku* 74, 1980, 67-88.

PANNONIA

Gorsium: Tác, near Székésfehérvár, Hungary

88. A bronze statuette, found in the *templum provinciae* during the excavations of 1970. Now, in the István Király Múzeum of Székésfehérvár, inv.
no. 70.166.1.

The statuette is executed in a style which portrays both considerable care
and considerable "barbarism" of concept. The artist was obviously not
trained in the classical style.

The divinity portrayed has a beard and moustache indicated by shallow incisions. His abundant hair is covered by a Phrygian cap, which has a decoration of incised lines and circles. The six circles (three on each side) closest to
the peak of the cap are so deep that they might have contained inserts (gems?).
The god makes the *benedictio Latina* with his right hand, and in his left holds
an indistinct object, perhaps a curled whip. He wears a tunic held at the waist
by a belt. Over the tunic he seems to wear a sleeved jacket, on which there are
numerous incisions indicating folds, and with a decorated band under the
neck and coming down both sides of the chest. The end of his belt, or perhaps
a sheath, falls down from his waist. The knees and lower legs are bare. He
wears boots held at the ankle by a wide band decorated with circular ornaments. On either side and behind, short appendages fall from the band, and
in front a long appendage extends from the band to the toe of each boot. All
are decorated with holes.

The figure stands on a square plate, which in turn rests on a hollow cylin-
drical base, originally equipped with four vertical handles (only one and part
of another are preserved). The handles must have served for the statuette to be
carried in some kind of ceremony. Interestingly enough, a figure of a feline, in
similar style and with a similar base, had previously been known from the
palatium of Gorsium. Both bases show holes unconnected with the handles.
(Cf. the nailholes on some Sabazius-hands, which allowed them to be fixed
on poles.)

Dimensions: height 0.145 (including base).

> Zsuzsanna Bánki, *La Collection du Musée Roi Saint Etienne, objets romains figurés
> en bronze, argent, et plomb*, Székésfehérvár 1972, no. 3; J. G. Szilágyi, *Le plastique
> de l'époque romaine en Pannonie, I-III siècle*, Székésfehérvár 1976, no. 25.

It would appear that this object was intended as a rein-guide and decorated
the front of a chariot, although it remains difficult even on this hypothesis to
explain its having four handles, not merely two. See M. Duchesne-Guillemin,

in U. Bianchi and M. J. Vermaseren (eds.), *La Soteriologia dei culti orientali nell'Impero romano*, EPRO 92, Leiden 1982, p. 168-70; *Bulletin de la Société Nationale des Antiquaires de France*, 1975, p. 76-92, and further bibliography cited there.

DUBIA

I do not propose to list here various items which have been, in my opinion, rather fancifully connected with Sabazius on iconographical grounds. I have dealt with them already in my article, "Towards a Definition of Sabazius-Iconography," in *Numen* 27, 1980, p. 9-33. Likewise I exclude various figurines and busts which combine a beard and a Phrygian cap, but have no more characteristic attribute of Sabazius. Nor do I propose to include certain problematical inscriptions which various authorities have hesitantly suggested to be connected with Sabazius, i.e., the two which mention a *theos Sabatikos* or *Sabathikos* (*Mouseion kai Bibliotheke* 3, 1880, p. 167, no. tle'; Keil and von Premerstein, *Zweite Reise*, pp. 117-8 no. 224) or that which mentions a college of *Sabbatistai* (*JHS* 12, 1891, pp. 233-6 = Dittenberger, *OGIS*, 573). With these items removed, we are left with a residue of only three monuments which have been connected with Sabazius with some probability, but without any claim to certainty.

Roma: Rome, Italy

D1. A typical relief of Mithras tauroctonus known since the 17th century. now in the Louvre, Paris, inv. no. 1023.
Dimensions: height 2.54; width 2.65.

> *CIL* VI, 719 and 30819; Cumont, *Textes et Monuments* II, no. 62; Vermaseren, *CIMRM* I, nos. 415-6, with other references.

The relief is accompanied by the following inscription:
    Nama Sebezio
    Deo Soli invict[o] Mitrhe
    C(aii) Aufidii Ianuarius [et.....]
    Nam-
5   a
    NECS

The presence of a representation of Mithras tauroctonus on the Sabazius-plaque no. 69 establishes a connection between these two cults, and lends probability to the connection of this piece with Sabazius. The similar piece *CIL* XIV, 3566, however, seems merely to be a Renaissance forgery. See Cumont, *Revue de Philologie* 1892, pp. 96-8.

Ancient name unknown: **Tekiya**, Jugoslavia
(on the Danube below Belgrade)

D2. A plaque of hammered silver, of which only the top part is preserved. It was found in excavating for the foundations of a building on June 12, 1948, and is now in the National Museum of Belgrade, inv. no. 2769. The preserved portion of the plaque shows us an aedicula with vegetative ornaments and rosettes in the pediment. Under it there is an apparently seated male divinity in 3/4 view. He is bearded and heavily clothed. In the field there are a winged caduceus and an insect of some sort. Perhaps the divinity held a patera. A plaque with Cybele or Demeter was found with this one. The identification as Sabazius can be backed up with reference to the attributes in the field, the fact that he is perhaps accompanied by Cybele, and the parallel furnished by the silver plaque no. 74 (which, incidentally, would never have been taken as representing Sabazius if it were not for the inscription). On the other hand, there is really nothing compelling from an iconographical standpoint in the identification nor is there any epigraphical confirmation.

Dimensions: height 0.095; width 0.11; weight 9.45 gr.

D. Mano-Zisi, *Nalaz iz Tekije*, Narodni Muzej Beograd, Antika 2, Beograd 1957, pp. 97-102 no. 35 and Pl. XXIV; Picard, *RA*, 1961 II, pp. 160-1 and figs. 11-12.

Philippopolis: Plovdiv, Bulgaria

D3. A stone stele in the form of a naiskos, now broken in two pieces. The circumstances of discovery are obscure, but it is now in the Plovdiv Museum, Inv. no. 3079. It has two registers. The upper one shows a divinity standing to the right, his left foot on an animal head, holding a thyrsus in his left hand and a pine-cone in his right, as if he were about to throw it. He has a beard, and wears a Phrygian cap and a tunic. Around him are smaller figures of Helios, Selene, Hermes, Pan, Tyche and others too indistinct to identify. The lower register is a fairly typical Thracian-rider relief, with some subordinate figures likewise. Although a Phrygian-capped Zeus-type has some prima-facie claim to be identified as Sabazius (cf. no. 52), the stance is unlike anything else which we have in Sabazius-representations, nor is there epigraphical confirmation.

Dimensions: height 0.37.

Picard *RA*, 1961 II, pp. 139-40 note 2 and fig. 5; Tatscheva-Hitova, no. 16; Tacheva-Hitova, *Eastern Cults*, no. IV 17.

TESTIMONIA ANTIQUA

1. Aristophanes, *Horae*, frag. 566:

> (τὸν) Φρύγα, τὸν αὐλητῆρα, τὸν Σεβάζιον

2. Idem, *Vespae*, 8-10. Sosias and Xanthias, the two slaves, are conversing:

> Ξα. ἀλλ' ἦ παραφρονεῖς ἐτεὸν ἢ κορυβαντιᾷς;
> Σω. οὐκ, ἀλλ' ὕπνος μ' ἔχει τις ἐκ Σαβαζίου.
> Ξα. τὸν αὐτὸν ἄρ' ἐμοὶ βουκολεῖς Σαβάζιον.
> κἀμοὶ γὰρ ἀρτίως ἐπεστρατεύσατο
> Μῆδός τις ἐπὶ τὰ βλέφαρα νυστακτής ὕπνος
> καὶ δῆτ' ὄναρ θαυμαστὸν εἶδον ἀρτίως.

3. Idem, *Aves*, 876. The priest is trying to sell his services, and identifies birds with gods:

> καὶ φρυγίλῳ Σαβαζίῳ καὶ στρούθῳ μεγάλη μητρὶ θεῶν καὶ ἀνθρώπων

4. Idem, *Lysistrata*, 387f. The Proboulos is speaking:

> ἆρ' ἐξέλαμψε τῶν γυναικῶν ἡ τρυφὴ
> χὠ τυμπανισμὸς χοἱ πυκνοὶ Σαβάζιοι
> ὅ τ' Ἀδωνισμὸς οὗτος οὑπὶ τῶν τεγῶν,
> οὗ 'γώ ποτ' ὢν ἤκουον ἐν τἠκκλησίᾳ.

5. Theophrastus, *Characters* 16, 4 (the Superstitious Man):

> καὶ ἐὰν ἴδη ὄφιν ἐν τῇ οἰκίᾳ, ἐὰν παρείαν, Σαβάζιον καλεῖν,
> ἐὰν δὲ ἱερὸν, ἐνταῦθα ἡρῷον εὐθὺς ἱδρύσασθαι.

6. Idem, *Characteres* 27, 8 (the Late Learner):

> ὁ δὲ ὀψιμαθὴς τοιοῦτός τις, οἷος .... τελούμενος τῷ
> Σαβαζίῳ σπεῦσαι ὅπως καλλιστεύσῃ παρὰ τῷ ἱερεῖ.

7. Cicero, *De Natura Deorum* 3, 23;

Dionysos habemus multos......tertium Cabiro patre eumque regem Asiae fuisse, cui Sabazia sunt instituta.

8. Idem, *De Legibus* 2, 15, 37:

Novos vere deos et in his colendis nocturnas pervigilationes sic Aristophanes, facetissimus poeta veteris comoediae, vexat, ut apud eum Sabazius et quidam alii dei peregrini iudicati e civitate eiciantur.

9. Diodorus Siculus 4, 4:

μυθολογοῦσι δέ τινες καὶ ἕτερον Διόνυσον γεγονέναι πολὺ τοῖς χρόνοις προτεροῦντα τούτου. φασὶ γὰρ ἐκ Διὸς καὶ Φερσεφόνης Διόνυσον γενέσθαι τὸν ὑπό τινων Σαβάζιον ὀνομαζόμενον, οὗ τήν τε γένεσιν καὶ τὰς θυσίας καὶ τιμὰς νυκτερινὰς καὶ κρυφίους παρεισάγουσι διὰ τὴν αἰσχύνην τὴν ἐκ τῆς συνουσίας ἐπακολουθοῦσαν.

10. Strabo 10, 3, 15:

καὶ ὁ Σαβάζιος δὲ τῶν Φρυγιακῶν ἐστι καὶ τρόπον τινὰ τῆς Μητρὸς τὸ παιδίον παραδοὺς τὰ τοῦ Διονύσου καὶ αὐτός.

11. Idem, 10, 3, 18:

τῶν μὲν γὰρ Βενδιδείων (ἱερῶν) Πλάτων μέμνηται, τῶν δὲ Φρυγίων Δημοσθένης διαβάλλων τὴν Αἰσχίνου μητέρα καὶ αὐτόν, ὡς τελούσῃ τῇ μητρὶ συνόντα καὶ συνθιασεύοντα καὶ ἐπιφθεγγόμενον "εὐοῖ σαβοῖ" πολλάκις καὶ "ὕης ἄττης, ἄττης ὕης". ταῦτα γάρ ἐστι Σαβάζια καὶ Μητρῷα.

12. Valerius Maximus 1, 3, 2, in the reading of Julius Paris' epitome according to Vat. Lat. 4929 (see Lane, *Journal of Roman Studies* 79, 1979, 35 ff.):

Cn. Cornelius Hispalus praetor peregrinus, M. Popilio Laenate, L. Calpurnio consulibus, edicto Chaldaeos citra decimum diem abire ex urbe atque Italia iussit, levibus et ineptis ingeniis fallaci siderum interpretatione quaestuosam mendaciis suis caliginem inicientes. Idem Iudaeos, qui Sabazi Iovis cultu Romanos inficere mores conati erant, repetere domos suas coegit.

The year referred to is 139 B.C.

13. Lucian, *Deorum Concilium* 9, Momus is teasing Zeus:

ἀλλ᾽ ὁ Ἄττης γε, ὦ Ζεῦ, καὶ ὁ Κορύβας καὶ ὁ Σαβάζιος, πόθεν ἡμῖν ἐπεισεκυκλήθησαν οὗτοι, ἢ ὁ Μίθρης ἐκεῖνος ὁ Μῆδος, ὁ τὸν κάνδυν καὶ τὴν τιάραν, οὐδὲ ἑλληνίζων τῇ φωνῇ, ὥστε οὐδ᾽ ἢν προπίῃ τις ξυνίῃσι;

14. Idem, *Icaromenippus* 27. The hero of the dialogue has arrived in heaven and takes part in a symposium of the gods:

καί με ὁ Ἑρμῆς παραλαβὼν κατέκλινε παρὰ τὸν Πᾶνα καὶ τοὺς Κορύβαντας καὶ τὸν Ἄττην καὶ τὸν Σαβάζιον, τοὺς μετοίκους τούτους καὶ ἀμφιβόλους θεούς.

15. Apuleius, *Metamorphoses* 8, 25. A crier, who is selling the donkey-hero to a priest of the Syrian goddess, is reviled by the priest:

At te, inquit, cadaver surdum et mutum delirumque praeconem, omnipotens et omniparens dea Syria et sanctus Sabadius et Bellona et Mater Idaea et cum suo Adone Venus caecum reddant, qui scurrilibus iamdudum contra me velitaris iocis.

16. Clemens Alexandrinus, *Protrepticus* 2, 15, 1ff. (p. 13, 2ff Stählin):

Σαβαζίων γοῦν μυστηρίων σύμβολον τοῖς μυομένοις ὁ διὰ κόλπου θεός. δράκων δέ ἐστιν οὗτος, διελκόμενος τοῦ κόλπου τῶν τελουμένων, ἔλεγχος ἀκρασίας Διός.

17. Artemidorus 2, 13:

καὶ θεοὺς πάντας (δράκων ὁρώμενος σημαίνει), οἷς ἐστιν ἱερός. εἰσὶ δὲ οἵδε, Ζεὺς Σαβάζιος, Ἥλιος, Δημήτηρ καὶ Κόρη, Ἑκάτη, Ἀσκληπιός, Ἥρωες.

18. Harpocration, s.v. Σαβοί:

Δημοσθένης ὑπὲρ Κτησιφῶντος. οἱ μὲν Σαβοὺς λέγεσθαι τοὺς τελουμένους τῷ Σαβαζίῳ, τουτέστι τῷ Διονύσῳ, καθάπερ τοὺς τῷ Βάκχῳ Βάκχους. τὸν δὲ αὐτὸν εἶναι Σαβάζιον καὶ Διόνυσόν φασιν ἄλλοι τε καὶ Ἀμφίθεος δευτέρῳ περὶ Ἡρακλείας. οὕτω δέ φασι καὶ τοὺς Ἕλληνας τινες τοὺς Βάκχους Σαβοὺς καλεῖν. Μνασέας δὲ ὁ Παταρεὺς υἱὸν εἶναί φησι τοῦ Διονύσου Σαβάζιον.

19. Origen, *Contra Celsum* 1, 9 incip.:

μετὰ ταῦτα προτρέπει (ὁ Κέλσος) ἐπὶ τὸ λόγῳ ἀκολουθοῦντας καὶ λογικῷ ὁδηγῷ παραδέχεσθαι δόγματα, ὡς πάντως ἀπάτης γινομένης τῷ μὴ οὕτω συγκατατιθεμένῳ τισί. καὶ ἐξομοιοῖ τοὺς ἀλόγως πιστεύοντας μητραγύρταις καὶ τερατοσκόποις, Μίθραις τε καὶ Σαβαδίοις καὶ ὅτῳ τις προσέτυχεν, Ἑκάτης ἢ ἄλλης δαίμονος φάσμασιν.

20. Iamblichus, *De Mysteriis* 3, 9 incip., talking about the effects of music:

ἃ δὲ λέγεις ἐπὶ τούτοις ἐστὶ ταῦτα -- ὡς τῶν ἐξισταμένων ἔνιοί τινες αὐλῶν ἀκούοντες ἢ κυμβάλων ἢ τυμπάνων ἤ τινος μέλους ἐνθουσιῶσιν, ὡς οἵ τε κορυβαντιζόμενοι καὶ οἱ τῷ Σαβαζίῳ κάτοχοι καὶ οἱ μητρίζοντες.

21. *Ibid.* 3, 10:

ἀλλ᾽ ἐπεὶ τῶν μὲν Κορυβάντων φρουρητική πώς ἐστιν ἡ δύναμις καὶ ἐπιτελεστική, τοῦ Σαβαζίου δ' εἰς βακχείας καὶ ἀποκαθάρσεις ψυχῶν καὶ παλαιῶν μηνιμάτων οἰκειότητα παρεσκεύασται, διὰ ταῦτα δὴ καὶ αἱ ἐπίπνοιαι αὐτῶν τῷ παντὶ διεστήκασιν.

22. Arnobius, *Adversus Nationes* 5, 20 f. After giving the same account as that in Clement, *supra* no. 16, the author continues:

ipsa novissime sacra et ritus initiationis ipsius, quibus Sebadiis nomen est, testimonio esse poterunt veritati (*sc.* of the preceding story), in quibus aureus coluber in sinum demittitur consecratis et eximitur rursus ab inferioribus partibus atque imis.

23. Firmicus Maternus, *De Errore Profanarum Religionum* 10:

Sabazium colentes Iovem anguem, cum initiantur, per sinum ducunt.

24. *Orphei Hymni*, no. 48, in Sabazium:

Κλῦθι, πάτερ, Κρόνου υἱέ, Σαβάζιε, κύδιμε δαῖμον,
ὃς Βάκχον Διόνυσον, ἐρίβρομον, εἰραφιώτην,
μηρῷ ἐγκατέραψας, ὅπως τετελεσμένος ἔλθῃ
Τμῶλον ἐς ἠγάθεον παρὰ Ἵπταν καλλιπάρηιον,
ἀλλὰ μάκαρ Φρυγίης μεδέων, βασιλεύτατε πάντων,
εὐμενέων ἀπαρωγὸς ἐπέλθοις μυστιπόλοισιν.

25. *Ibid.*, no. 49, in Hiptam, 1f.:

Ἵπταν κικλήσκω, Βάκχου τροφόν,
εὐάδα κούρην, μυστιπόλον, τελετῆσιν
ἀγαλλομένην Σάβου ἁγνοῦ.

26. Macrobius, *Saturnalia* 1, 18, 1:

Item in Thracia eundem haberi solem atque Liberum accepimus, quem illi Sebadium nuncupantes magnifica religione celebrant, ut Alexander (*sc.* Polyhistor) scribit: eique deo in colle Zilmisso aedes dicata est specie rotunda, cuius medium interpatet tectum.

27. Proclus, *In Platonis Timaeum* 3, 41, 10 f. Diehl:

παρειλήφαμεν καὶ παρὰ Φρυξὶ Μῆνα Σαβάζιον ὑμνούμενον ἐν μέσαις ταῖς τοῦ Σαβαζίου τελεταῖς.

28. Hesychius, s.v. Σαβάζιος:

ἐπώνυμον Διονύσου. οἱ δὲ υἱὸν Διονύσου. καὶ Σάβον ἐνίοτε καλοῦσιν αὐτόν. Φρὺξ δὲ ὁ Σαβάζιος.

29. Damascius, *In Platonis Parmenidem* 160 (2, 44, 3 f. Ruell):

ἕνωσις μὲν δημιουργικὴ ὁ μονοειδὴς εἷς δημιουργός. ὁλότης δέ, ὁ ἤδη μὲν τὰ μέρη προφαίνων, οὔπω δὲ μεριζόμενος, οἷος ὁ Σαβάζιος. ὁ δὲ Διόνυσος τὸ ἄπειρον ἤδη μεριζόμενον πλῆθος.

30. Johannes Lydus, *De Mensibus* 4, 51 (pp. 106-7 Wünsch):

Τερπανδρός γε μὴν ὁ Λέσβιος Νύσσαν λέγει τετιθηνηκέναι τὸν Διόνυσον τὸν ὑπό τινων Σαβάζιον ὀνομαζόμενον, ἐκ Διὸς καὶ Περσεφόνης γενόμενον, εἶτα ὑπὸ τῶν Τιτάνων σπαραχθέντα.

31. Photius, *Lexicon*, s.v. Σαβοί:

Σαβοὺς καὶ Σαβὰς καὶ Σαβαζίους τοὺς βακχεύοντας τῷ Σαβαζίῳ. ὑπὸ δέ τινων ὁ Διόνυσος Σαβὸς καλεῖται.

32. Souidas, s.v. Σαβάζιος:

ὁ αὐτός ἐστι τῷ Διονύσῳ. ἔτυχε δὲ τῆς προσηγορίας ταύτης παρὰ τὸν γινόμενον περὶ αὐτὸν θειασμόν. τὸ γὰρ εὐάζειν οἱ βάρβαροι σαβάζειν φασίν. ὅθεν καὶ τῶν Ἑλλήνων τινὲς ἀκολουθοῦντες τὸν εὐασμὸν σαβασμὸν λέγουσιν. ἔνθεν Σαβάζιος ὁ Διόνυσος. Σάβους ἔλεγον καὶ τοὺς ἀφιερωμένους αὐτῷ τόπους καὶ τοὺς Βάκχους αὐτοῦ.

33. Michael Psellus, *De Verborum Significatione*, p. 109 Boissonade:

ἔστι ὁ μὲν Ἄττις τῇ Φρυγίᾳ γλώσσῃ ὁ Ζεύς, τὸ δὲ ὕις εὐκτικόν ἐστι, τὸ δὲ σάβα ἐθνικόν. ὥστε τὴν ὅλην εὐχὴν τοιαύτην εἶναι "ὕις ὦ Ζεῦ Σαβάζιε, ὕις."

34. *Etymologicum Magnum, s.v.* Σαβάζιος:

ὁ Διόνυσος, διὰ τὸν γινόμενον περὶ αὐτὸν θειασμόν. τὸ γὰρ εὐάζειν οἱ βάρβαροι σαβάζειν λέγουσιν. ὅθεν καὶ τῶν Ἑλλήνων τινὲς ἀκολουθοῦντες τὸν εὐασμὸν σαβαζμὸν προσηγόρευσαν.

35. *Etymologicum Gudianum* s.v. Σαβανδιός (p. 495 Sturzius):

ἐπώνυμον Διονύσου.

36. Eustathius, *in Odysseam* 1431, 45 f (II. 16):

ἡ Ῥέα, ᾗ φασιν ὁ κατεχόμενος ἢ καὶ ἄλλῳ δαίμονι καταχρηστικῶς, κύβηβος ἐλέγετο. ὁ καὶ σάβος καὶ Σαβάζιος καὶ Βάκχος καὶ βαβάκτης καὶ βάβαξ, κτλ.

37. Idem, *In Iliadem* 1078, 20 f (XVI, 617), talking about various dances:

ἦν δὲ καὶ σίκιννις, κωμικωτέρα (τῆς πυρρίχης), ἣν πρῶτον, φασὶν, ὠρχήσαντο

Φρύγες ἐπὶ Σαβαζίῳ Διονύσῳ, ὀνομασθεῖσαν κατὰ τὸν Ἀρριανὸν ἐπὶ μιᾷ τῶν ὀπαδῶν τῆς Κυβέλης νυμφῶν, ᾗ ὄνομα ἦν Σίκιννις.

38. *Scholia in Aristophanis Vespas* 9 and 12:

πρὸς τὸ κορυβαντιᾷς εἶπε τὸ Σαβάζιον......Σαβάζιον δὲ τὸν Διόνυσον οἱ Θρᾷκες καλοῦσι, καὶ Σαβοὺς τοὺς ἱεροὺς αὐτῶν.
Μῆδός τις ἢ πρὸς τὸ Σαβάζιος εἶπε καὶ οὗτος τὸ Μῆδος ἢ ἄνευ τοῦ ἐχθρός κτλ.

39. *Scholia in Aristophanes Aves* 874:

καὶ φρυγίλῳ Σαβαζίῳ. παίζει πρὸς τὸ ὄνομα, ἐπεὶ οἱ Φρύγες Σαβάζιον τιμῶσι. τίς δέ ἐστιν οὗτος ὁ θεὸς ὁ Ἡρακλεώτης (Ἀμφίθεος) περὶ Ἡρακλείας ἐν τῷ β΄ φησὶν οὕτως, "φαίνεται γὰρ ἐξ ὧν εὑρίσκομεν συλλογιζόμενοι πολλαχόθεν ὅτι Διόνυσος καὶ Σαβάζιος εἷς ἐστι θεός, τυχεῖν δὲ τῆς προσηγορίας ταύτης παρὰ τὸν γινόμενον περὶ αὐτοῦ θειασμόν. τὸ γὰρ εὐάζειν οἱ βάρβαροι σαβάζειν φασίν, ὅθεν καὶ τῶν Ἑλλήνων τινὲς ἀκολουθοῦντες τὸν εὐασμὸν σαβασμὸν λέγουσιν."
ἄλλως, παίζει πρὸς τὸ ὄνομα, ἐπεὶ Φρύγες τὸ εὐάζειν σαβάζειν φασὶ καὶ ἐκ τούτου Σαβάζιον τὸν Διόνυσον λέγουσι. σάβους δὲ ἔλεγον καὶ τοὺς ἀφιερωμένους αὐτῷ τόπους καὶ τοὺς βάκχους τοῦ θεοῦ.
ἄλλως, ἐπεὶ Φρυγῶν ὁ θεός. καὶ ἐν Ὥραις "τὸν Φρύγα, τὸν αὐλητῆρα, τὸν Σαβάζιον."

40. *Scholia in Aristophanis Lysistratam* 388:

Σαβάζιοι, οἱ ὀργιασμοὶ τοῦ Σαβαζίου, ὃν οἱ μὲν τὸν αὐτὸν τῷ Διονύσῳ ὑπειλήφασι. τυχεῖν δὲ τῆς προσηγορίας ταύτης διὰ τὸν γινόμενον περὶ αὐτὸν εὐασμόν. τὸ γὰρ εὐάζειν οἱ βάρβαροι σαβάζειν ἔλεγον. ὅτι δὲ εἷς ἐστιν ὁ θεὸς Σαβάζιος καὶ Διόνυσος πολλοὶ μαρτυροῦσι κωμικοί.

TESTIMONIA ANTIQUA DUBIA

Here I list two passages which are frequently cited as providing evidence about Sabazius, but not, to my way of thinking, entirely convincingly. I confess, however, that my doubts go against the majority opinion, especially in the cases of the first passage, which has been connected with Sabazius at least from the time of Strabo (cf. *supra* no. 11).

D1. Demosthenes, *De Corona* 259-60, trying to defame Aeschines:

ἀνὴρ δὲ γενόμενος τῇ μητρὶ τελούσῃ τὰς βίβλους ἀνεγίγνωσκες καὶ τἄλλα συνεσκευωροῦ, τὴν μὲν νύκτα νεβρίζων καὶ κρατηρίζων καὶ καθαίρων τοὺς τελουμένους καὶ ἀπομάττων τῷ πηλῷ καὶ τοῖς πιτύροις, καὶ ἀνιστὰς ἀπὸ τοῦ καθαρμοῦ κελεύων λέγειν "ἔφυγον κακόν, εὗρον ἄμεινον," ἐπὶ τῷ μηδένα πώποτε τηλικοῦτ' ὀλολύξαι σεμνυνόμενος (καὶ ἔγωγε νομίζω. μὴ γὰρ οἴεσθ' αὐτὸν φθέγγεσθαι μὲν οὕτω μέγα, ὀλολύζειν δ' οὐχ ὑπέρλαμπρον), ἐν δὲ ταῖς ἡμέραις τοὺς καλοὺς θιάσους ἄγων διὰ τῶν ὁδῶν, τοὺς ἐστεφανωμένους τῷ μαράθῳ καὶ τῇ λεύκῃ, τοὺς ὄφεις τοὺς παρείας θλίβων καὶ ὑπὲρ τῆς κεφαλῆς αἰωρῶν, καὶ βοῶν "εὐοῖ σαβοῖ," καὶ ἐπορχούμενος "ὑῆς ἄττης ἄττης ὑῆς," ἔξαρχος καὶ προηγεμὼν καὶ κιττοφόρος καὶ λικνοφόρος καὶ τοιαῦθ' ὑπὸ τῶν γρᾳδίων προσαγορευόμενος, μισθὸν λαμβάνων τούτων ἔνθρυπτα καὶ στρεπτοὺς καὶ νεήλατα, ἐφ' οἷς τίς οὐκ ἂν ὡς ἀληθῶς αὐτὸν εὐδαιμονίσειε καὶ τὴν αὐτοῦ τύχην;

D2. Plutarch, *Symposium* 4, 6, 2:

οἶμαι δὲ καὶ τὴν τῶν Σαββάτων ἑορτὴν μὴ παντάπασιν ἀπροσδιόνυσον εἶναι. Σάβ-βους γὰρ καὶ νῦν ἔτι πολλοὶ τοὺς Βάκχους καλοῦσι καὶ ταύτην ἀφιᾶσι τὴν φωνὴν ὅταν ὀργιάζωσι τῷ θεῷ.

TOPOGRAPHICAL INDEX

(The listing is by present-day place-name, and excludes Dubia and pieces of unknown provenience.)

MUSEUM INDEX

(An asterisk indicates that an item is no longer to be found)

EPIGRAPHICAL INDEX

I. RES SACRAE (EXCEPTO IPSO SABAZIO), REGES, IMPERATORES, ET ALIA VERBA NOTABILIORA, INCLUSIS NOMINIBUS GEOGRAPHICIS

Ἀγνούσιος - 51
Ἀδριανὸς Καῖσαρ - 21, 24
Ἀθηνᾶ - 27
Ἀθηναία - 28
Ἀθυπαρηνός - 1
Αἰγινίτης - 51
Αἰθαλίδης - 51
Ἀλιμούσιος - 51
Ἀλωπεκῆθεν - 51
Ἀμαξαντεύς - 51
Ἀμφιτροπῆθεν - 51
Ἀναγυράσιος - 51
Ἄνγδιστις - 31
Ἀντιοχεύς - 51
Ἀπαμεύς - 51
Ἀρσεληνός, Ἀρσιληνός - 10, 16, 17
Ἄρτεμις Ἀνάειτις - 33
ἀρχιερεύς - 11
Ἀχαρνεύς - 51
Αὐδναῖος μήν - 34
(Βασιλεὺς) Ἀρταξέρξης - 31
Βασιλεὺς Ἄτταλος - 27
βασιλεὺς Θρακῶν - 10
Βασίλισσα Στρατονίκη - 27
βοηθὸς χορνιχουλαρίων - 2
βουλευτής - 16
γραμματεύς - 51
Δαίσιος μήν - 41
δένδρα θεῶν - 33
Δῆλος - 48
Δῖος μήν - 27
ἔνπυρα - 31
ἐπήκοος - 2, 4, 6, 7, 17
ἐπιμελητής - 12, 51
ἐπιμήνιος - 46
ἐπιστάτας - 46
ἐπίτροπος - 43
Ἕρμειος - 51
Εὐμενὴς φυλή - 30
Ζεύς - 3, 8, 9, 10, 21, 22, 24, 25, 27, 29, 30, 32, 33, 34, 36, 37, 38, 39, 40, 41, 42, 43, 45, 48, 53, 55
    Ζεὺς Βαραδάτης - 31
    Ζεὺς Ἥλιος - 16
    Ζεὺς Κορυφαῖος - 42
Ἡρακλεώτης - 51
Θεὰ Ἰδεία Μεγάλη - 16
Θεὰ Σ... - 30

Θίασος Σαβαζιανός - 6
ἱερεύς - 1, 3, 6, 11, 30, 41, 43, 51, 54, 55
    ἱερεὺς Ἀπόλλωνος - 48
    ἱερεὺς Δήμητρος καὶ Σαοάσου - 44
    ἱερεὺς Διονύσου - 43
    ἱερεὺς Ἑρμοῦ - 43
    ἱερατεύων - 43, 44a
ἱερόδουλος - 34, 36
κατ' ὄνιρον, κατ' ὀνείρου ἐπιταγήν - 22, 45
Κιβυράτης - 43
Κικκυνεύς - 51
κοινόν - 6
    κοινὸν τῆς ἐπαρχείας - 11
    κοινὸν Σαβαζιαστᾶν - 46
Κολοηνῶν κατοικία - 41
Κολωνῆθεν - 51
Κυρείνα - 11
κύριος - 1, 5, 7, 12, 16
Λ. Σεπτίμιος Σεουῆρος - 10
    Σεουῆρος - 23
Λαοδικεύς - 51
λεγεὼν β´ Παρθική - 5
Λυδία - 31
Λυκίων ἔθνος - 44a
Μ. Αὐρ. Ἀντωνῖνος Σευῆρος - 4
    Μ. Αὐρ Ἀντωνῖνος Καῖσαρ - 10
    Ἀντωνῖνος - 23
Μᾶ - 31
Μαίων - 42
Μακεδών - 51
Μαρωνίτης - 51
Μεσορὴ μήν - 50
Μήτηρ Ἵπτα, Μήτηρ Εἵπτα - 36, 37, 40
Μητρικός - 2
Μιλήσιος - 51
μισθωτής - 43
Μουνιχιὼν μήν - 51
μυστήρια, μύσται - 27, 31, 43
ναός - 1, 10
Ναυλίτης - 42
Νέρουας Τραειανὸς Καῖσαρ - 22
Νικηφόρος (Ἀθηνᾶ) - 27
Ξυπεταιών - 51
Ὄαθεν - 51
Ὀῆθεν - 51
οἶκος καὶ περικείμενος ψιλὸς τόπος - 39
Οἰναῖος - 51
Ὀρμηλέων δῆμος - 43

II. NOMINA RELIQUORUM VIRORUM ET MULIERUM

Νίκων - 52
Ξενοκλείδης - 51
Οἴμηδος - 3
Ὀνησιφόρος - 54
Ὀσαίς, Ὀσαείς - 43
Πάρος - 64
Παυλεῖνος - 6
Πιείσεισος - 12
Πλούταρχος - 51
Πλουτίων - 42
Πόθων - 51
Πολέμαρχος - 51
Πολέταρχος - 55
Πόπλιος - 4, 55
Πόρος - 6
Ποσειδώνιος - 43
Ῥόδιππος - 51
Ῥοῖμος - 3
Ῥοῦφος - 48
Σεῖος - 22
Σῆλος - 6
Σήραμβος - 51
Σκέλος - 11
Σοφεῖνος - 6
Στρατόνεικος - 33
Σύμμαχος - 43
Σωμένης - 51
Σωσιγένης - 51, 52
Σῶσος - 51
Σωτᾶς - 51
Τάρσας - 3
Τειμοκράτης - 22
Τιβέριος - 43
Τῖτος - 11
Τρόφιμος - 34, 36, 40
Φαῖδρος - 51
Φαυστεῖνα - 43
Φείλιος - 2
Φιλόστρατος - 51
Φίλων - 51
Φιλωτέρα - 26
Φλάουιος - 11, 16
Χρῆστος - 8
Ὠκυμένης - 51
...αλος - 3
...κενθος - 3
...σίαλος - 35
Aelius - 57
Aemilius - 66
Alexander - 61, 62
Antullus - 69
Attia - 58
Aufidius - D1
Aulus - 60
Aulusanus - 71
Aurelius - 19, 20, 57, 59, 75

Bassus - 57
Bonus - 57
Caecilius - 60
Caerellius - 70
Carassounus - 74
Celerina - 58
Celerinus - 18
Cessicus - 14
Clarus, Clara - 59
Cleme(n)s - 13
Diogenes - 57
Ennius - 18
Eperastus - 56
Euschemus - 66
Faustus - 57
Felicissimus - 67
Flavius - 3, 57
Furius, Furia - 59
Gaius - 74
Germanus - 75
Hiberus - 68
Ianuarius - D1
Iulianus - 14
Iulius - 57, 74
Longinus - 57
Luccius - 68
Lucius - 20, 56, 66, 67, 68
Marcellinus - 19
Marcianus - 20
Marcus - 15, 18, 59, 70, 73, 75
Mercator - 71
Mestrius - 57
Mettius - 72
Mucianus - 57
Nunnius - 61, 62
Oppius - 73
Pegasus - 58
Pistus - 57
Plotius - 56
Pompeianus - 13, 57
Pompeius - 67
Quintus - 61, 62
Servilia - 63
Servilius - 15
Severus - 57
Sossius - 70
Statius - 72
Sudius - 57
Valens - 57
Valentinus - 57
Valerius - 71
Verecundus - 15
Vibia - 65
Victor - 57
Vincentius - 65
Vitalis, Vitalius - 57, 73
Zethus - 72

III. MONUMENTA QUORUM CERTA VEL QUASI CERTA EST AETAS

ACKNOWLEDGEMENTS OF THE ILLUSTRATIONS

1. Photo after Mihailov, *IGBulg.*
2. Photo after Mihailov, *IGBulg.*
3. Photo after Mihailov, *IGBulg.*
4. Photo after Mihailov, *IGBulg.*
5. Photo after Mihailov, *IGBulg.*
7. Drawing after Mihailov, *IGBulg.*
9. Photo after Mihailov, *IGBulg.*
10. Photo after Mihailov, *IGBulg.*
11. Photo after Buvukliev, *Arkheologija* 7, 1965.
12. Photo after Mihailov, *IGBulg.*
13. Photo after Zotović, Les cultes orientaux sur le territoire de la Mésie Supérieure.
16. Photo after Mihailov, *IGBulg.*
17. Photo after Mihailov, *IGBulg.*
18. Photo after Tacheva-Hitova, *Eastern Cults.*
19. Photo after Macrea, *Dacia* 3, 1959.
20. Photo after Macrea, *Dacia* 3, 1959.
21. Photo after Dörner, *Inschriften und Denkmäler aus Bithynien.*
22. Photo after Dörner, *Inschriften und Denkmäler aus Bithynien.*
23. Photo after Robert, *Hellenica* 7, 1949.
25. Drawing after Cook, *Zeus.*
26. Photos courtesy Deutsches Archäologisches Institut, Ausgrabungen zu Pergamon.
27. Photo courtesy Staatliche Museen zu Berlin (-Ost)
30. Photo after Johnson, *Religions in Antiquity.*
31. Photo after Robert, *CRAI*, 1975.
32. Drawing after Keil and von Premerstein, *Zweite Reise.*
36. Photo after Herrmann, *Ergebnisse.*
37. Drawing after Keil and von Premerstein, *Zweite Reise.*
41. Drawing after Cook, *Zeus.*
42. Photo after Keil and von Premerstein, *Zweite Reise.*
44a. Drawing after *TAM* II.
45. Photo after Cook, *Zeus.*
46. Photo courtesy Vassa Kontorini.
47. Photo by author.
48. Photos after Vatin, *BCH* 91, 1967.
51. Photo courtesy Epigraphiko Mouseio, Athens.
52. Photo courtesy Epigraphiko Mouseio, Athens.
54. Photos by author.
57. Photos by author.
58. Photo by author.
59. Photo by author.
60. Photo by author.
61. Photos courtesy Detroit Institute of Arts.
65. Drawings after Nilsson, *Geschichte der griechischen Religion.*
66. Photo by author.
73. Photo after Mahjoubi, *CRAI*, 1960.
74. Drawing after Cook, *Zeus.*
76. Photo courtesy British Museum, London.
77. Photo courtesy Rudolf Fellmann.
78. Photo courtesy Universitea din Bucureşti, Institutul di Arheologie.
79. Photo by author.
79a. Photo courtesy Rudolf Fellmann.

80. Photo after Blinkenberg, *Archäologische Studien*.
81. Photo courtesy Staatliche Museen zu Berlin (-Ost).
82. Drawing after Bonner Jahrbücher 23, 1856.
83. Photo after Nilsson, *Geschichte der griechischen Religion*.
84. Photo after Nilsson, *Geschichte der griechischen Religion*.
85. Drawings after Garcia y Bellido, *Les Religions orientales dans l'Espagne romaine*.
86. Photos courtesy Musée du Louvre, Paris.
87. Photos courtesy Archaeological Museum, Zadar.
88. Photos courtesy István Király Múzeum, Székésfehérvár.
D1. Photo after Vermaseren, *CIMRM*.
D2. Photo after Mano-Zisi, *Nalaz iz Tekije*.
D3. Photo after Picard, *RA*, 1961.

PLATES

PLATE I

1

2

PLATE II

3   4

5

PLATE III

```
ΚΥΡΙωϹΕΒΑΖ
ΕΠΙΚωΜΑΡΧ
ΜΟΥ      ΚΕΡ
  ΑΙ     ΟΥ
ΕΘΘΙΚΛΙΜ
ΚΟΥΒΕΛΙΟΥ
ΕΝΟΙΤΟ
```

7

9

10

PLATE IV

11

12

PLATE V

16

13

PLATE VI

18

17

PLATE VII

20

19

PLATE VIII

Plate IX

PLATE X

23

25

PLATE XI

26b

26a

PLATE XII

PLATE XIII

30

31

PLATE XIV

35

36

PLATE XV

40

39

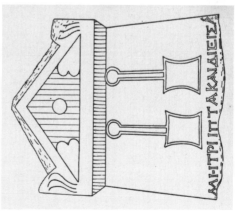

37

PLATE XVI

41

PLATE XVII

45

42

PLATE XVIII

46

PLATE XIX

47

48a

48b

PLATE XX

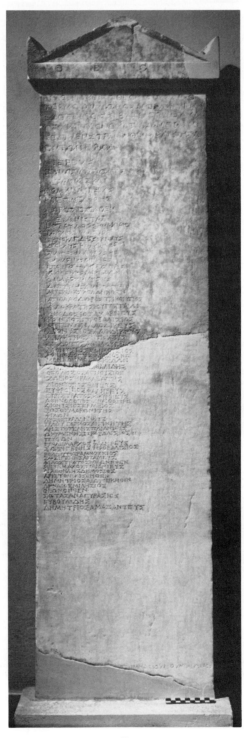

PLATE XXI

52a

52b

PLATE XXII

54a

54b

PLATE XXIII

57a

57b

PLATE XXIV

57c

57d

PLATE XXV

58

59

60

PLATE XXVI

61a

61b

61c

PLATE XXVII

a)

b)

c)

d)

PLATE XXVIII

66

73

PLATE XXIX

74

76

77a

77b

PLATE XXX

78

PLATE XXXI

44.

PLATE XXXII

80

79a

PLATE XXXIII

82

81

PLATE XXXIV

84

83

PLATE XXXV

85a

85b

Plate XXXVI

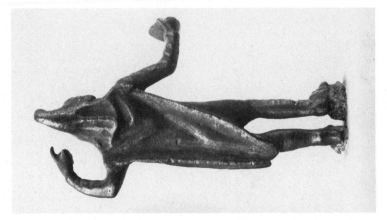

86d

86c

86b

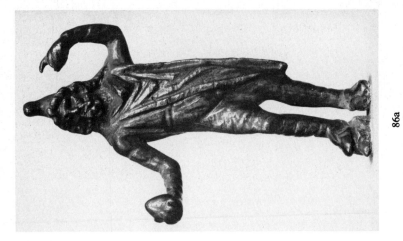

86a

PLATE XXXVII

PLATE XXXVIII

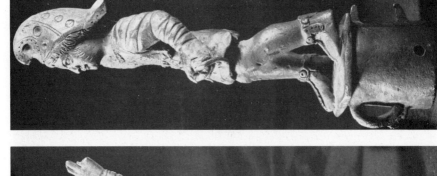

88d

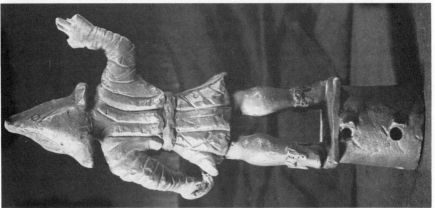

88c

88b

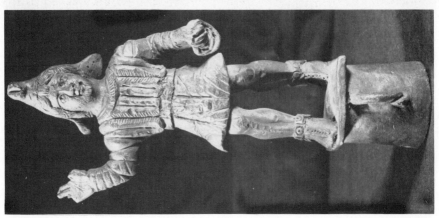

88a

PLATE XXXIX

D1

PLATE XL

D3

D2

F.E. Derksen-Janssens 1985

MOGONTIACUM

RHAETIA

NORICUM

GORSIUM

DACIA

PANNONIA

DACIA SUP.

POTAISSA

INF.

APULUM

SUP.

INF.

ITALIA

Fintinele

LUNA

AENONA

MOESIA

MUNICIPIUM

MOESIA INF.

JADAR

DALMATIA

TIMACUM MINUS

MONTANENSIUM

Turgovishte

Pirot

Pavlikeni

NICOPOLIS AD ISTRUM

Dragoman

VOLSINII

Mramor

Buhovo

PHILIPPOPOLIS

Viterbo

Maslovo

SERDICA

AUGUSTA TRAIANA

BITHYNIA

PONTUS

ROMA

Fiano Romano

SUP.

Javorovo

OSTIA

Capranica Prenestina

PAUTALIA

Isakcilar

ARMENIA

CASINUM

MACEDONIA

SPORTELA

THRACIA

DACIBYZA

Karamanli Camii

GALATIA

SUESSULA

SYLLANTA

CAPPADOCIA

BLAUDOS

EPIRUS

PERGAMUM

SAITTAE

AUGUSTAPOLIS

COMMAGENE

Ayazviran

KOLOIDA

Sandal

COLOE

ASIA

MAIONIA

PHILADELPHIA

GRAECIA

SARDIS

LYDIAE

CILICIA

SYRIA

TEOS

ATHENAE

EPHESUS

PIRAEUS

ORMELEIS

EPIDAURUS

DELUS

Aglanköy

ARGOS

TLOS

BELALIS MAJOR

SICINUS

THERA

RHODUS

FRICA

CYRENAICA

AEGYPTUS

OXYRRHYNCHUS

BELGIC

GALLIA
LUGDUNENSIS

GER

.AQUAE CALIDAE

GALLIA

GALLIA
NARBONENSIS

TARRACONENSIS

EMPORIAE

LUSITANIA

BAETICA

MAURITANIA

NUMIDIA

CORPUS CULTUS IOVIS SABAZII

(CCIS),II THE OTHER MONUMENTS

0   100   200   300   400   500 km